www.tredition.de

AF196911

Furtado-Brum / Meneses

Azorean Legends as Folklore

www.tredition.de

© 2015 Regina Oberschelp de Meneses

Verlag: tredition GmbH, Hamburg

ISBN
Paperback: 978-3-7323-7581-3
Hardcover: 978-3-7323-7582-0

Printed in Germany

Azorean Legends as Folklore

Foreword/Introduction:

Stories and legends tell us of times long gone by. But have they preserved their relevance for the understanding of modern life in the Azores? They depict through exemplary case studies the attitudes of the settlers as they found themselves facing overwhelming natural forces, primarily those of the heaving and breathing ocean surrounding the islands, as well as those resulting from unpredictable earthquakes and erupting volcanoes. Bewilderment joined fear, heightened by the isolation of the nine small islands in the vastness of the Atlantic Ocean. Far away from the continents, the islanders had to constantly be prepared to ward off outside attacks, whether man-made or of climatic influence. At the same time, the new immigrants had to develop and uphold a working society based on ethical values that through mutual assistance could ensure a secure lifestyle and guarantee a viable chance of survival in the face of the uncertainties surrounding the islands. The individuals in this interdependent group structure were left to adjust to their challenging environment by allowing their imagination to search for new limits in the supernatural spheres in order to try to grasp the unexplainable, while at the same time struggling to come to terms with the geographically restricting confines.

Once an important hub connecting worlds of difference in the vastness of the Atlantic Ocean, their influence still extends to Azorean communities in faraway places on all continents. At the same time, the archipelago continues to harbor unexpected secrets amidst the looming threats that have not ceased to hover around the tiny specks of volcanic rock, just waiting to be discovered.

From rough rock formations, they have matured into nine gemstones sparkling in the velvety blue waters. Each island is characterized by a defining color: the yellow amber Santa Maria, the green emerald São Miguel, the blue sapphire Faial, the grey pyrite Pico, the brown carnelian São Jorge, the white diamond Graciosa, the lilac amethyst Terceira, the pink ruby Flores, and the lucky obsidian Corvo.

The islands all vary in size and are differently faceted, and yet are bound together by their experience of mutual interdependence, offering a shared history with nine faces. To be prepared for the unexpected, to discover the secrets of the Azores, past and present, the visitor should take some time to delve into the past - not as the history books tell it, but as the people tell it through their unforgettable stories and legends. So, follow me, if you please.

The Azorean Archipelago

The creation of the Azores

Many, many years ago, there was a land where brooks were gurgling with crystal-clear water, while the vegetation would cushion every step you took through its lush abundance. The air was drenched with the sweet scent of flowers, and their colorful petals sparkled in the dazzling landscape. In this paradisiacal country, nine brothers distinguished themselves from the general populace by their sheer natural beauty and wisdom. They were also the best of friends and helped one another whenever necessary.

Together they used to climb the highest peaks to survey the lovely landscape stretching out at their feet. Over time, each of the nine brothers showed a preference for a particular hilltop. Somehow each one of them became convinced that the soil on the peak that he had chosen happened to be more fertile, the vegetation lusher, than those on the other elevations.

One day, they decided to approach the king and ask him to grant them permission to settle in their preferred domains. The benevolent king kindly responded: "Dear sirs, I bequeath to you the nine mountaintops you desire so that you may prosper there and enrich the land." The nine brothers were delighted and wasted no time in arranging their new estates. However, before they parted, they embraced and agreed to reunite once a year, because they were, after all, the best of friends and were certain to miss one another's company.

The nine brothers had no sooner moved to their new properties, when powerful tremors started to shake the land. The ocean waters churned in turmoil, and waves the size of mountains climbed the coast and rushed through the unfortunate valleys, devouring everything in their path.

After the relentless fury of the sea finally subsided, only the peaks the nine brothers had chosen dazzled in a newly found tranquillity, rising out of the deep blue ocean. The mountaintops were now islands, and they are still inhabited by the descendents of the nine wise brothers. Today we know them as the Archipelago of the Azores.

It is indeed surprising how, year after year, the climatic biosphere described in this legend manages to reawaken the archipelago's inhabitants to gain a new lease on life. During the harsh winter months, the overpowering Atlantic Ocean seems to orchestrate a grim water funeral. Especially in the first three months of each year, all terrestrial life threatens to be dragged to the bottom of the sea. Water drips from saturated foliage, water seeps through the porous volcanic rock and rushes to the relentlessly swelling ocean, taking soil, structures, and even lives with it that obstruct its path. Ferociously the waves rise to the size of mountains, aimed at conquering and devouring the land. White foam on black lava stone proves to be a fatal attraction for whoever approaches the fascinating spectacle without taking proper caution. On the rising cliffs, fog engulfs the water-drenched mosses and lichen.

And then the sun breaks through the hopeless grey of an apocalyptic sky. Feathery clouds sail over playfully leaping white horses. From the celestial blueness, the sun seems to wink down: "For better or for worse – but beware of the eternal secrets of the sea!"

The princess of Atlantida

A long time ago, when the nine islands of the Azores were still connected in a single land mass forming the formidable kingdom of Atlantida, the ruling king had one absolutely charming daughter. Although the father loved the princess, his predominant concern always rested on the well-being of his kingdom. In order not to jeopardize its state of harmonious equilibrium, he forbade his daughter to even contemplate any frivolous distractions, among them, falling in love or marrying.

However, as life will have it, a dashing prince in shining armor came by and swept the princess off her feet. The upright daughter decided not to deceive her father and resolutely asked for an audience. The king did not believe his ears when his daughter told him straight out that she intended to abdicate her kingdom in order to marry the intrepid gallant.

At first perplexed, the king's surprise turned into hatred, and in a blind rage, he sought the help of a magician. Quivering with rage, the king ordered him to transform his unsuspecting daughter into a tree, to be planted in the cavalier's property. The magician conceded, but he secretly added that if as much as a twig on that tree suffered harm, the kingdom of Atlantida would be inundated and disappear into the ocean within an instant.

When the young man learned of his beloved's plight, he devoted his days to wrapping his arms around the tree trunk, disregarding wind and weather, sun and rain. After a while it occurred to him that if he broke off a twig and carried it inside his shirt, his long-lost love would always be close to his heart.

However, no sooner did he hold the broken-off twig in his hand, when the earth began to shake and the sound of gushing waters filled the valleys of Atlantida. In no time the kingdom was flooded and submerged in the ocean, with only its peaks peering out of the water.

Thus, the fabled reign of Atlantida came to its mysterious end. And nothing was left behind but the nine mountain tops, which, nowadays, we know as the nine islands of the Azores. Of course, the first Azorean settlers were not aware of the fact that the frightening natural forces they witnessed were caused by shifting tectonic plates under the flexible soil they stood on. However, imaginative stories managed to distract from the wild winds chasing around the small stone houses, while their inhabitants huddled around the flickering fireplaces.

Now and again, the islands shake and tremble in nights when the full moon turns the sea into livid silver. Everybody who cares to listen clearly hears the moaning sigh of the princess of Atlantida who lost everything, her beloved and her kingdom.

São Miguel

The princess and the shepherd

In São Miguel, the larger of the two islands in the southeastern extremity of the Azorean archipelago, there was a fabled kingdom in "Sete Cidades" of immense riches, displaying a truly glamorous lifestyle. The ruling king was the proud father of one daughter, whose beauty, intelligence and gentleness was unsurpassed by any other girl in his realm. This princess loved to frolic through the lush pastures and fields full of abundant crops, while listening to the twittering birds in the blue sky and the murmuring brooks in the cooling shadow of whispering trees.

One day, the blue-eyed princess was ambling through the country-side, singing a sweet song of yearning and love, when, all of a sudden, she met a shepherd sitting under the canopy of an ancient tree, tending his flock. His green eyes were sparkling with good humor while they talked animatedly about the flowers and the animals in this amiable bucolic setting. When evening came, they had fallen deeply in love with one another. So in the following weeks, they regularly met in the protective shadow of the giant tree trunk.

Inevitably, the king came to know about his daughter's clandestine encounters, and he was anything but pleased because he had arranged for her to marry the prince of a neighboring kingdom. As is not surprising, the sovereign forbade his daughter to pursue this ill-suited relationship. The princess knew quite well that it would do no good to try to change her father's mind. Therefore, she contented herself with asking for the king's permission to allow her to meet the shepherd one last time.

As principled as the sovereign was, just as much did he love his only daughter. He allowed the lovers to meet one last time under the sheltering canopy of the old tree. They knew that they would not be able to see each other again, and their tears flowed abundantly until they formed two distinctive lakes at their feet. One was blue and the other one green.

Today, the lakes still remind us of the tragic love between these two young lovers. Side by side, the Lagoa Azul, with its waters as blue as the sparkling eyes of the vivacious princess, and the Lagoa Verde, shimmering green like the eyes of the jilted shepherd. There are no kings residing in São Miguel nowadays; the times of slaves are long gone by. But the names of the old nobility still stick out among those of relatively common descent. If you, as a tourist, inadvertently omit to pay the proper respect, that still raises an eyebrow or two on their part – and leaves the onlookers watching with amusement. Social barriers might have corroded, but tragic love-stories still break hearts, also in São Miguel.

How Rabo de Peixe got its name

Rabo de Peixe, or Fishtail in Portuguese, is a small fishing village on the northern coast of the Azorean island of São Miguel. Many a curious visitor has approached the patient inhabitants to find out the curious origin of this unique place name. And yet, the explanation is so simple. The response reaches well back into the middle of the 15th century, which provides it with the necessary veneration.

In the early days of the first settlements, this low and fertile land attracted as much attention as the amazing abundance of fish in the sea lapping at its shore. Life was easy-going, and the fishermen always found time to sit at the waterfront and drift off in idle small talk while scrutinizing the far horizon.

One day, some fishermen were passing the time of day, talking about nothing in particular, when they quite unexpectedly found themselves engaging in a heated discussion about which name should befit their sprouting settlement. Nobody was meant to be offended, and yet, nobody quite felt like submitting to somebody else's opinion.

In order to avert a clashing confrontation among friends, one fisherman decided to interrupt the intensifying brawl: "Hey, you would not believe it! I know what to call our parish: Fishtail. Look at that over there!"

Two days earlier, a small fish had been spotted by a large predator fish and ended up flitting around with such erratic movements that it tore itself into two pieces, one part heading in one direction, the other one shooting away in another.

After a moment of puzzled silence, roaring laughter greeted the man's unexpected suggestion. When the explosive mirth finally died down, the fishermen found themselves watching the fishtail bobbing peacefully on the rippling waves. Surprised contemplation settled in. A name such as Fishtail would not be regarded as an offense or favoritism by any in their midst. Besides, the name sounded fitting for a parish whose livelihood was largely provided for by the wide Atlantic Ocean.

And thus the inconspicuous little settlement in the middle of fertile fields and abundant fish stocks grew to become one of the most populous places in São Miguel. It still bears the name Rabo de

Peixe. And the fishermen still gaze at the water after work is done, whiling away the time. They no longer need to occupy themselves with finding a suitable name for their location. Nowadays, the cooling beer bottles are used to garner peace between the supporters of the two major Portuguese football clubs, Benfica and Sporting. But in the end, everybody agrees that there is no better team than the local one: Santa Clara, olé!

Lagoa Seca, the lake with and without water

Many years ago, there was a village called Lagoa Seca, dry lake, close to Furnas on the Azorean island of São Miguel. One day, its population was boisterously celebrating a special holiday, when one woman had to get water from the village well. To her greatest surprise, her jug filled with steaming hot water mixed with sandy gravel, instead of the customary cool spring water. The woman became terrified and rushed to her husband to tell him and their friends celebrating around him what had happened. However, nobody wanted to listen to her. And what is more, the woman even had to endure the unabashed scorn of the tipsy crowd. None of them seemed to notice that the sky had turned dark prematurely, although nightfall had not yet come. By now, the woman was in a panic and, envisioning a terrible punishment, tried to physically pull her husband away from the festivities. But he simply did not want to budge.

When she saw that all her frantic efforts were in vain, she fled all by herself, driven by a terrible premonition. No sooner had she reached the first hilltop, when she turned around, trying to catch her breath. Instead, the sight took her breath away. The calm waters of an extensive lake stretched out at her feet, as if it had always been there. Nobody would imagine that at its bottom rested her village, Lagoa Seca, with all of her relatives and friends. Bewildered, she scanned the silent water. Right in front of her, the waves licked at a Holy-Spirit-crown and a Holy-Spirit-sceptre rolling around forlorn on the grassy shore.

At first, the perplexed woman did not know what to do. Then, she gathered up the crown and the sceptre and proceeded in the direction that the Holy-Spirit-dove pointed. Just before reaching Ponta Garça, the bereaved woman stumbled into the chapel of Nossa Senhora das Mercês. Completely exhausted, she reverently placed the crown and the sceptre on the altar and knelt down to pray.

Today, the Holy-Spirit-crown and Holy-Spirit-sceptre can still be seen where she left them. The village of Lagoa Seca remains hidden for all eternity under the still waters of the Lagoa das Furnas.

However, even nowadays the inhabitants residing amidst the burbling sulphur wells seem to be completely oblivious to the fabled health inducing sulphur fumes. Any tourist ambling by feels embarrassed by irreverently contemplating how long the offensive smell of foul eggs will linger in his or her holiday attire.

A mud hole named Pêro Botelho

Many years ago, there lived in Furnas an evil man, who was called Pêro Botelho. He was well-known and much-feared for his violent and explosive temperament. Like many other people living in this part of São Miguel, he often had his food boiled in one of the seething hot mud holes. On cold winter days, he could sometimes be seen huddling in their vicinity, as the sulphur vapors are said to cure all kinds of ailments, including rheumatism.

One day, Pêro Botelho was seen close to the edge of one of the most turbulent mud holes. Maybe he had been tasting too much of the young wine that day, for it was the harvest season. Or the devil might just have felt the need for a conspiratorial chat with a like-minded soul. In any case, Pêro Botelho slipped into the bubbling mud and disappeared for good without uttering another swear-word. He never emerged again, and until the end of time, you can hear him shouting: "Take me out of here! Take me out of here!"

Still today, the villagers approach this mud hole with the greatest care and respect, for it continues to spit out little pieces of rock amidst billowing clouds of smoke. Beware! Pêro Botelho is just waiting for you to join him.

The magic island of Nordeste

Once upon a time, a magical island was lying just in front of the rugged coastline of Nordeste, the northern tip of the Azorean island of São Miguel. It was a fabulous island where eternal summer sun and the gentle spring breezes caressed the lush meadows and the fertile fields. Its inhabitants lived in gilded palaces and the king's daughter was the most beautiful princess there ever was. Every day she ambled through the blessed island, turning every man's head with her golden curls and sparkling blue eyes. Yet, consistently, she turned every marriage proposal down.

One day, a richly ornamented ship arrived in the island's natural harbor with a serious looking delegation whose sole purpose was to ask the king for his daughter's hand. In a far-away country, the mighty ruler of a vast empire had no doubts about his request being granted, as nobody had ever dared to confront him. When his messengers came back empty-handed, he felt so offended by the princess's rejection that he flew into a terrible rage. Imperiously, he swore to take revenge and ordered a complying witch to cast a damning spell.

The enchanting island in front of Nordeste was sent to the bottom of the sea. Every seven years, it arises in the night of São João, St John's Eve. Ghostly white fog veils float around it, while its translucent contours are desperately waiting to be released from the spiteful spell. When one listens to the unruly waves hitting the rough coastline of Nordeste, one can still hear the charming princess inconsolably bemoaning her cruel fate.

Thanks to the subtropical weather conditions in June, the fascinating fog formations over the open sea invite every onlooker to let his or her fantasy run wild. Well, you can actually see the island right over there ... or can't you?

King D. Sebastião and the enchanted island

Less than 100 years ago, the inhabitants of the Azores still had to fetch from springs and wells all the water they needed for washing and cleaning, for the watering of plants and animals as well as for the preparation of food. All too often, one had to wait in line to fill one's jugs, which, of course, was ideal for those trading the latest village gossip. However, some people preferred to use the cooler nights to avoid the tongue-lashing crowds.

The two Bastos sisters from Ribeira Seca de Ribeira Grande on São Miguel were among those who usually tried to avoid wasting time. One night, they found themselves alone at the well, filling their water jugs while listening to the far-away waves in the peaceful silence, dreamily surveying the whispering sea glittering in the mysterious silvery light of the full moon.

All of a sudden, a long path emerged from out of the water's depth, and, in a full canter, a majestically clad young man on a fiery white horse came galloping straight up to them. He reigned in his impatiently whinnying stallion and asked in a pleasant voice: "Who is alive?"

At first, the two women held their breath in utter surprise. Then, they clasped their water jugs to their chests and, while the noble horseman asked the same question twice more, they dashed home, terrified by the unexpected appearance. As they turned their heads back one last time, just before reaching the safety of their house, they were surprised to see the disappointed rider trotting back on the path he had come so vigorously. His head bowed, his shoulders drooped, and behind him the path disappeared in the twinkling waves.

The next day, the Bastos sisters told their neighbors about their strange encounter. Everybody seemed to understand instantly that it had been the fabled King Don Sebastião who had approached them for help, hoping to free his enchanted island from the unrelenting spell. The sisters were now, belatedly, told that they should have answered: "Don Sebastião and his nation." Those words would have changed their tragic fate. Yet, at the same moment, Don Sebastião´s island would have been released from the fateful magic, another Azorean island, one bearing a female name, would have seen itself cast under the dreadful spell in its turn.

Until today, Don Sebastião has not succeeded in shrugging off his ill-begotten destiny, and, thus, every seven years, the desolate king rises out of the water and hopes to find somebody to set his island free. That, of course, makes the inhabitants on the little island of Santa Maria, in plain view off the south shore of São Miguel, tremble in their knees. However, do they really need to worry? In June, the biggest Azorean island, São Miguel, is full of tourists discovering the natural and historic beauties of the Azores. And Don Sebastião would either have to repeat his request in English and German, or be condemned to wait another seven years.

The maidens' marsh

In Covoado there is an isolated bog which was called maidens'
marsh for longer than anyone cares to remember. When the full
moon dispenses its cold light over the treacherous site, translucent
nymph-like creatures come floating from afar to wash their shimmering white clothes in the silver-colored waters. To dry them,
they fastidiously spread them over the green tufts of grass, and then
they dance and sway to inaudible tunes and melodies in a most
graceful manner, their feet never touching the ground.

Just before the magic moonlight gives way to the awakening colors
of dawn, the nymph-like creatures collect their clothing and disappear in all wind directions – only to reappear when the full moon
beckons for another friendly gathering in the maidens' marsh.

The warning of the Ribeira da Mulher

Although this story happened more than 400 years ago, everybody
in Nordeste remembers why the brook Ribeira da Mulher received
its name, the River of the Woman. At that time, a young man from
São Miguel had to sail to the neighboring island of Santa Maria to
conduct some business. During his short stay there, he inadvertently fell in love with a sprightly young woman, whose blazing red

hair and sparkling green eyes fatefully bedazzled the otherwise happily married man.

Laden not only with a favorable business deal, but also with a guilty conscience, he returned to his native village of Povoação in São Miguel, not knowing that the enamored young woman would follow him. Relatives and friends were shocked when they found out about the young man´s escapades in the neighboring island, and their disapproval turned to hateful persecution of the young lovers.

The adulterous young man saw no choice but to flee with his dismayed beauty from Santa Maria to the remote part of Nordeste. For a while, they lived off the fruits of the forest, until the young woman could not bear the desperate situation any longer. Without a glimmer of hope in sight, she broke down and cried so much that she dissolved into a gurgling brook rushing to the ocean. Grieving his fleeting love, the young man realized he had lost not only his family and honor but also his true love. He broke down and drowned himself in the brook that is still called Ribeira da Mulher – and everybody, at least in Nordeste, still understands its murmuring message and eternal warning.

Among the predominantly Catholic population, breaking one's marriage vows is still not considered an acceptable pastime, while the maiden's marsh allows for uncensored daydreaming and night fantasies. Just like in the Bible, no doubt remains as to who is to blame for the tragedy. Just a hint: it is not the man.

The rivals' cave

Once upon a time, two brothers lived in the village of Mosteiros on the Azorean island of São Miguel. They were of equal strength and courage and, as such, highly respected by one and all, not least of all because they even behaved justly and fairly when fighting their rivals. Inseparable in work and play, they were regarded with sincere respect, and every young girl blushed at their sight and included them in her marriage plans.

However, as chance would have it, they lost their hearts to the very same girl. From one day to the next, their friendship and amiability dissipated and gave way to suspicious distrust and unreasonable loathing. In accord, they each went to great lengths to avoid each other's company at work and at play.

One fateful Friday evening, they accidentally met at a narrow stretch of the road close to the cave of Mosteiros, both on their way to the house of their mutual sweetheart. They instantly began to attack each other. At first, they exchanged words that, in their appalling lack of respect, they would never even have thought up in former days. Then, fists flew, and, finally, they pulled out their weapons. Both of them were equally strong, both of them were equally determined, both of them were struck by the lethal blows at the same moment, each slain by the hand of his brother.

The din of the struggle lured the girl out of her nearby home. When she reached the gruesome scene, she fell to her knees, the blood of the two brothers staining her clothes. Desperately, she wrung her praying hands up to the sky full of sparkling stars, and her wailing joined the mournful last breaths that united the two brothers again, this time in death.

Every Friday evening, when the wind causes the waves to crash high against the rocks of Mosteiros, above, the agitated storm birds shriek in lamenting voices. Only when the church bells chime at midnight, does silence return to the towering rocks. The shadow of a praying woman slips across their rugged surface, as the clouds obscure the cold moonlight at the Gruta dos Rivais.

And then there are visitors who think nothing ever happens in the Azores. Yet, even at night, life pulses in harmony with the ever swelling ocean tides.

The bewitched fruitcake

Not quite 100 years ago, a solitary woman lived with her daughter in the Azorean village of Mosteiros on the island of São Miguel. She was said to be knowledgeable in the art of witchcraft, but when her daughter was reaching marriageable age, a young man braved all the rumors and became good friends with the girl.

However, her mother soon had enough of waiting for him to propose to her daughter and decided to resort to some witchcraft to help persuade him to declare his honorable intentions. She cleverly kneaded the dough to make fruitcake on the bare bosom of her co-operating daughter. When the pastry came out of the oven, its smell was so tantalizing that one´s stomach involuntarily started to growl and grumble.

Soon the young man came by to pay his daily visit after work. Eagerly, the mother offered him an exceptionally big slice of fruitcake, which he could hardly resist. Yet, he became suspicious because both women were goggling at him so intently. To placate them, he assured them that he wanted to save the delicacy for on his way home, while resolutely ignoring the hunger pangs that were gnawing at his intestines.

At dusk, he bid his customary farewell, and when he was out of sight and around the next corner, he offered the fruitcake to a donkey that was tethered in front of a neighbor's house. As soon as the greedy animal had gulped down the bewitched food, it broke loose and, in a highly agitated state, galloped to the house the young man had just left. In front of it, the usually docile animal burst out in a cacophony of braying that made the whole neighborhood come running.

The astonished young man had followed at a distance. Enraged, he now shouted above the heads of the crowd: "Did you really want to see me like this?" Mother and daughter stayed behind closed windows. Their efforts had missed their target considerably. They never set eyes on the young man again, nor did any other suitor ever show up either; with that result, I wonder why?

The shoemaker's well

Many years ago, a shoemaker living in Ginetes had to go to Ponta Delgada in order to deliver the shoes he had made and to buy new leather and get new customers. While his wife, who was at that time suffering from bowel problems, was handing him the food for the trip, she asked him to get her a specific medication a neighbor had recommended to cure her ailment.

After the long and tiring walk to town, the shoemaker was happy to meet old acquaintances and exchange the latest news with them. He then took the shoes to his customers and gladly received new orders. Afterwards, he still had to buy suitable leather before he could embark on his home journey. It had been a long day, and he was already contemplating how to make the new shoes he was supposed to deliver as fast as possible.

Just before he reached the outskirts of Ginetes, he suddenly remembered his wife's errand. Befuddled, he stopped in his tracks and considered his options. If he were to turn back and get the medication in Ponta Delgada, he would never make it home before nightfall. However, returning home without the requested elixir did not look like an appealing prospect either.

At first disheartened, he ponderously scanned the landscape. Suddenly, he perceived a gurgling well, practically hidden in the lush green vegetation at the wayside. The shoemaker's head shot up, for a desperate idea had struck him. He carefully cleaned his water container which he then filled with the fresh well water.

At home, his wife had been eagerly waiting for him to tell her the latest news from town. All too happily, he obliged, and then he handed her his water container, with anguish in his heart. In the following days, the water of the well was used sparingly, as the shoemaker's wife fastidiously followed her neighbor's instruction. Slowly, but surely, her bowel affliction subsided, and the shoemaker's guilty conscience made him confess the truth about his water container.

Word spread fast, and soon people from Ginetes used the water of the Fonte do Sapateiro, the "Shoemaker's Well," to try to cure any ailment that plagued them. Today, the medicinal properties of this water are no longer recognized by everybody, but its main purpose remains. The water still quenches the thirst of anyone wandering by, including that of the cows peacefully grazing nearby.

The marriage well

In the village of Furnas on the Azorean island of São Miguel, a sweetly murmuring spring breaks through the lush vegetation on Pico de António Borges and gurgles into a refreshing basin on the left side of the bridge. This water is renowned for its increasing magical influence over the summer months on all those who drink from it before the first ravaging autumn storms break its spell. Whoever tastes its water, inexplicably and inadvertently, falls in love, and therefore it is known as the "marriage well."

One summer, a noble family from Ponta Delgada decided to evade the stifling August heat by temporarily moving to the cooler surroundings of Furnas. Their only daughter had already spent some time here and in Rosto de Cão, under the surveillance of a doctor, in order to improve the fragile health she had been born with. Yet, the girl, descending from well-to-do families that adhered to the strict principle of only agreeing to arranged marriages befitting their upper-class status, had never overcome her sickly nature. For 20 years, which was her exact age, she had been engaged to a cousin 10 years her senior. However, the young man, of equally illustrious descent, was so feeble-minded that it was rather doubtful if he would ever be able to support himself, let alone a wife and family.

Stormy weather seemed to be looming close to the Azores, because even in Furnas the humidity felt quite unbearable. Therefore, the noble family resorted to spending a day on Pico de António Borges. Yet, even at this altitude, no considerable cooling effect offered any relief. Lethargically, the listless daughter plucked a leaf from a nearby bush and used it to scoop water out of the well to quench her thirst.

All afternoon long, she had been watching a merry party of farmers from Bretanha, a rural area in São Miguel where settlers from Brittany and Flanders did not devote their time to worry about social class systems. They were enjoying themselves boisterously, dancing and singing, while the most delicious food smells appealed to the young girl's olfactory sense. And there, an energetic young man approached the basin, breathing heavily after all the exuberant hopping and shouting he had engaged in all day long. Eagerly, he grasped the very leaf that the young noblewoman had just discarded and heartily appreciated the cooling spring water trickling down his parched throat. Suddenly, and quite unexpectedly, he felt irresistible passion well up in him. Likewise, the pale cheeks of the timid town girl blushed in healthy excitement, with neither of the two young people understanding what was happening to them.

When, after some days of cooling rain showers, the young man returned with his relatives to his village in Bretanha, the young noblewoman left with him. Outraged, her father sent his servants after them. However, they had to return empty-handed because she was already happily married by the time they found her. The sickly young woman overcame her poor health, and like a delicate rose after a refreshing summer shower, blossomed to unexpected beauty – thanks solely to the magic water of the cooling marriage well.

As one can see, the ancestry of the Azorean population does by no means reflect a true image of their bureaucratic Portuguese nationality. Many customs, traditions, names and dishes still prove today that the original population was a fair mix of hard-working refugees from Brittany and Flanders, and noble Portuguese loyal to their king who was commanding a world empire at that time.

The Franciscan monastery in Lagoa

At the end of the 17th century, the Franciscan brotherhood decided to build a monastery in Lagoa on the Azorean island of São Miguel. Unfortunately, the order did not own any land in the area, and so one of the monks was put in charge of acquiring a suitably sized plot. He wasted no time and presented himself to the Capitao Donatário, the administrator of the island, and humbly asked him if he would consider donating some land to the poor monks. The administrator saw no reason why he should not give a helping hand to the needy brotherhood, and asked about the area required for constructing the monastery. Perhaps the Franciscan feared that his demand would be rejected if he exceeded the expectations of the administrator, as he therefore very humbly requested a plot of land no bigger than that which could easily be bounded by a cow´s skin.

The administrator thought the phrasing of the monk's request was slightly odd, but did not take time to question it. Magnanimously, he confided in the cleric and wasted no time to have his consent put in writing. Joyfully, the monk returned to his brethren and instantly proceeded to cut a cowhide into one long ultrathin leather strip that they then used as measurement to eagerly encircle the plot chosen to build their monastery.

In order to see how far a slender strip of cowhide can take you, enjoy a visit to the well-kept town garden of Santa Cruz da Lagoa. It now stretches where the Franciscan monks once built their first monastery. The monastery was later moved to another plot, north of where it first stood.

The legend of the Santo Cristo

A long time ago, the nuns at the convent of Caloura on the Azorean island of São Miguel became distraught, since they regretted that the inhabitants of the nearby village of Água de Pau were turning their backs on religious beliefs. Desperately, they continued to pray for the villagers' spiritual salvation, but nobody paid any attention to them.

Finally, the nuns decided that they needed to regain the people´s attention in order to rebuild their religious faith. They sent a petition to the Pope in far-away Italy, humbly asking him to supply them with a new statue, as they themselves did not have the financial resources to afford one.

Either their request became lost during the voyage, or the Holy Father was too busy with more important matters, or he was in financial difficulties himself; in any case, the disappointed nuns received neither reply nor statue.

At this point, strangely enough, it was not the Pope, but pirates who came to the nuns' assistance. For centuries, these wild sailors spread fear and destruction in the Azorean islands as well as in the surrounding sea. They looted and rampaged villages and merchant ships alike. Whatever they could not use, they discarded or burned. Many a merchant ship sank to the bottom of the sea, its cargo washing ashore as welcome flotsam on the Azorean islands.

One evening, some nuns finally straightened up after having spent all day bending down to tend their crops in the convent´s vegetable garden, which was so important to the mere survival of the humble religious community. With strained faces, they were surveying the receding tide, when, suddenly, their tired eyes came to rest on a big box stuck between the wet boulders of the stony beach. Curiosity got the better of their exhaustion, and in a joint effort, they managed to pull the wooden container onto dry shore.

When they opened its lid, all tiredness left them as they clasped their soiled hands to their mouths to stifle their excited shrieks of amazement. From inside the box, a man-sized bust of Christ the Savior smiled at them with a benevolent expression of peaceful serenity. Elated, the nuns created a place of honor for the bust in their convent´s chapel.

News soon spread, and the curious inhabitants of Água de Pau came to hear mass again, while goggling at the astonishing find supplied by the waves of the mighty ocean. Quickly, rumor spread that the Santo Cristo was working miracles. Slowly, but surely, the whole population of São Miguel flocked to the convent of Caloura to pay respect to the statue of the Santo Cristo.

In the meantime, the nuns became increasingly intimidated by the frequent pirate attacks around their convent in Caloura. In the end, they fled to take refuge in the Convento da Esperança in Ponta Delgada, not without having the Santo Cristo accompany them.

Nowadays, the procession in honor of the Santo Cristo on the 4th Sunday in May is attracting many faithful as never before. However, one wonders how many of those pilgrims realize that they should be grateful to loathsome pirates, because without their intervention, Azorean Catholics would not have their cherished religious festivity in honor of Senhor Santo Cristo dos Milagres.

The eternally blooming rosary

In the 16th century, the abbess Teresa da Anunciada devoted her life in the Convento da Esperança to praying and funding a new chapel built for the statue of the much venerated Senhor Santo Cristo dos Milagres.

One year, though, the Azorean island of São Miguel was plagued by an extensive drought, and Madre Teresa had a hard time keeping the roses, carnations and marguerites alive in the convent´s garden. She needed these flowers not only to adorn her beloved Santo Cristo, but also to sell them so that the building of the new chapel for the statue could advance. One Wednesday morning, Madre Teresa got up early, as was her custom, and went to her flower patch to see whether the cuttings she had left in a water container the previous Sunday were ready to be planted. To her utter amazement, one of the sprigs had produced a most beautiful rose. She instantly cut it off and added it to the flower decoration of the Santo Cristo. There it gave off such a tantalizing fragrance that everybody kneeling at the statue could not help but look at the rose admiringly. A few days later, more buds opened, convincing the nuns that this was indeed a special rose.

At the end of her life, one that she had so diligently devoted to the convent's flowers, Madre Teresa was called to heaven. Yet, the rosebush can still be seen in the peaceful garden of the Convento da Esperança. Its blossoms do not only continue to adorn the statue of Senhor Santo Cristo dos Milagres, but they are also handed to patients in the hospital of São José, where their fragrance spreads instant hope and consolation.

The white dove

In 1673, a terrible plague raged through the Azorean island of São Miguel during the Lenten season. The death toll was particularly high in the town of Ponta Delgada where once the Grim Reaper had entered a house, he did not feel inclined to leave until the last member of the family had been taken to the cemetery.

In their desperation, some of the noble families finally turned to a fortune teller, called Lucas, who used to read the future by watching the star constellations. This man predicted that the power to stop the epidemic by the grace of God lay in the hands of a pure girl from Ponta Delgada.

The extremely pretty but rather simple girl turned out to be 20-year-old Cristina de Gusmão, who had fled to an isolated house near Capelas, where she spent her days fervently praying for the plague to end. One day, an immaculately white dove came gliding down to perch right in front of the anxiously praying girl. From its cooing, Cristina understood that she was to sew a banner with the dove and the symbols of the Holy Trinity on it. She was then supposed to carry it through the streets of the town.

The influential families of Ponta Delgada listened to what Cristina told them and founded the Society of the Império dos Nobres. On that first Saturday after Easter, they carried the first banner symbolizing the Holy Spirit in a solemn procession through the streets of Ponta Delgada. The very same day, the epidemic stopped claiming new victims, and most of the sick suddenly felt stronger and began to get better.

Out of gratitude to the Holy Spirit, a special mass was said at the altar of São Roque in the Igreja Matriz, the main church of Ponta Delgada. Quite unexpectedly, an immaculately white dove came gliding in through the open church door. It circled the interior of the church three times, and three times it sat down to rest, first on the frieze of a chapel, then on the pulpit and finally on the main altar. After the religious ceremony, the dove left through a gabled window, the congregation reverently watching the bird's flight.

Nowadays, these extraordinary events are still remembered on the "Monday of the Little Dove," the first Monday after Whit Sunday. In Azorean life, the dove continues to be regarded as the most important symbol of religious belief, representing the Holy Spirit. These days, the Monday after Whit Sunday is the Azorean national holiday.

The holy bird Lavandeira

It was a beautiful day in July at the time of the early settlements on the Azorean islands, during the 15th century, when two women, mother and daughter, called Teresa and Isabel, were kneeling in front of a freshly tended grave in a cemetery on the Azorean island of São Miguel. Their faces were marked by their deep sorrow over the death of their beloved husband and father.

All of a sudden, a yellow-grey bird flew in and perched right in front of them, wagging its tail and inclining its head, and intently observing the two women. To their greatest amazement, it then commenced to speak, for it had come as the personification of the archangel Michael, who is the patron saint of the biggest Azorean island: "I want you to tell the people that God chose me to protect the Virgin Mary and the child Jesus and after they had to flee from Egypt, I erased their tracks with my tail. Furthermore, remind the people that I am indispensable for keeping the crops in the fields free of insects so that there will be enough food for everyone."

After having delivered this message, the delicate wagtail wagged its tail again and flew away. At first, mother and daughter were too perplexed to move. Then, they got up, rushed home and told all of their friends and neighbors about their astonishing encounter. As the two women were held in high regard, the news spread fast. And while little songbirds often became included in the Azorean cuisine as special treats, the endemic Azorean wagtail, lovingly called Avelinha or Lavandeira, was never added to this sad list of culinary delicacies. It became known as a sacred bird, never to be chased or killed, as happened to many other birds.

The chapel of Nossa Senhora da Vitória

At the end of the 16th century, the Azorean islands suffered innumerable attacks by Muslim pirates roaming the Atlantic Ocean all the way from northern Africa to Iceland. In those uncertain times, the commander of the castle of Angra on the island of Terceira sent his rather pretty young daughters to stay in the convent of Santo

André in Vila Franca on the island of São Miguel. They were not meant to join the convent as nuns, their father just wanted them to receive the much-appreciated education of the wise nun Maria de São Boaventura.

Shortly before the completion of their learning and their return to Angra, the younger daughter had a terrible nightmare in which she and her sister were dragged aboard a pirate ship to become slaves. Fortunately, the nun Maria de São Boaventura possessed the gift of reading the future and interpreting dreams. Therefore, she calmed the girl down and promised that the Virgin Mary would grant the two sisters a safe voyage home to Angra. Besides, it was not the ship, but Vila Franca that would be attacked by the pirates. However, with the help of Nossa Senhora da Vitória the population would prevail and repulse the marauding pirates.

The last Sunday before the sisters were supposed to sail home, the convent rejoiced in festive celebrations. Two pirates, Sali and Ibraim, mingled in the crowd. Their mission was to find lucrative targets for the pirates to loot. Their father had been the ruler of a Mauritanian dynasty, but when he was killed by Christian crusaders, his sons had sworn to avenge him and had joined a crew of pirates. They were highly educated and spoke various languages, including Portuguese.

As soon as they laid eyes on the two Azorean sisters, the two Muslim brothers instantly lost their hearts to them, without the girls suspecting anything. When, at night, the pirates planned their attack to ransack Vila Franca, Sali and Ibraim followed their own train of thought, having only the beautiful sisters in mind.

In the middle of the following night, the corsairs stormed into Vila Franca. The drowsy inhabitants, among them the nuns with their charges, awoke in time to escape with their bare lives into the rugged interior of the island. The Mauritanian pirates sacked Vila Franca, but Sali and Ibraim did not take part in the looting. Instead, they concentrated on looking for the two sisters who had so unwittingly stolen their hearts.

When the befuddled inhabitants gathered their wits and perceived the havoc the pirates wreaked, they became furious. Resolutely, they grabbed sticks and branches and whatever they managed to find in the darkness and swooped down on the unsuspecting marauders. Heavily laden with provisions and riches, the pirates rushed to the harbor, only to find that a fresh wind had agitated the waves and that their little boats had drifted away so that they could not reach their ship. Recognizing their advantage, the inhabitants of Vila Franca fought ferociously, never showing restraint. Only a few pirates managed to escape by the skin of their teeth as they threw themselves into the heaving waves. Sali and Ibraim died in a puddle of blood and never saw the two young girls return to Terceira safe and sound.

In Vila Franca, the street in which the population shouted "Vitória! Vitória!" after this audacious defense is still called Rua da Vitória. The little chapel erected to thank the Virgin Mary was destroyed long ago, but an inscription above a house entrance still reminds us of its site.

Santa Maria

The coquettish Garrida

At the end of the 16th century, Christopher Columbus returned from his first voyage to the New World that later came to be known as America.

As soon as he reached Azorean waters, one of those ravaging winter storms churned up the Atlantic, keeping the nine islands as much in suspense then as they still do today. Columbus recognised that he had to reach a safe harbor just as soon as possible because his caravel Niña was reduced to ping-ponging on the mountainous crests of the powerful ocean waves. The crew desperately tried to reach the Bay of Cré at the island of Santa Maria, but the mooring became shredded to pieces, and the Niña was again pushed against the coast. The sailors already feared their hour had come, as the crashing waves stripped the caravel of everything that could move on deck. Even the ship´s bell, called Garrida, which roughly translates as coquetry, was swept overboard and sank to the bottom of the bay.

When the storm at last calmed down, Columbus wasted no time in leaving Santa Maria. Yet, his Garrida, the coquetry, he had to leave behind. On sunny summer days, one can easily distinguish its contours from any ordinary fishing boat. In the clear water, colorful fish nibble at it as if they wanted to kiss it, but the bell will never frighten them with its ringing.

The captured wine-grower and the chapel of Nossa Senhora dos Prazeres

It was the season of the wine-grape harvest on the Azorean island of Santa Maria, and a wine-grower chose to guard his isolated vineyards at the outer edges of the Faja da Maia. He was worried that dogs, goats or even thieves would steal his grapes before he got a chance to pick them. His wife and children spent a restless night in their humble house in Calheta, as they were well aware that on occasion pirates had chosen to attack the island on that coastline.

Early the next morning, one of the daughters was to take food for that day to her father, and as she came skipping down the shortcut between Calheta and the Faja da Maia, she suddenly saw that their vineyards lay devastated, the chapel of Nossa Senhora dos Prazeres completely destroyed. Petrified, the girl dropped her food basket and then rushed to the place where she had last seen her father. She ran back and forth and called his name – to no avail.

It did not take long for the news to spread that the wine-grower had been kidnapped by pirates, an occurrence that had happened so many times before on this small island in the middle of the Atlantic Ocean. The bells of the four neighboring villages chimed for his wellbeing. Fifteen years passed, and the wine-grower's family continued to live in their humble cottage in Calheta, without ever overcoming the shock of the violent capture of their husband and father.

One night, when everybody had been safely tucked away in their beds, somebody knocked, with an urgency, on the front door. The mother called to her sons to check whether there was a neighbor outside who needed their help. The young men obediently left their warm beds and glanced outside. All of a sudden, they became wide awake and hastened to their mother. With bated breath they whispered that there was a Muslim with a long beard and tousled hair waiting at their door.

Enraged, the boy's mother jumped out of bed and equipped all of her children with broom sticks and firewood planks. Hatred threatened to quell her voice as she urged them: "I don't want you to spare him! No Muslim is ever to enter this house!" With revenge on their minds, the children slid out the back door and surprised the patiently waiting figure in his billowing robes before he could escape. They attacked him from all sides, bludgeoning him mercilessly. He collapsed and whimpered in pain: "Spare me! I am not a Muslim, but your father! Call your mother to identify the leaf-shaped birthmark I have on my left shoulder blade!"

Apprehensively, the children's mother approached the stranger, and to her greatest surprise, she could verify that he really was her long-lost husband. After all these years of anguish and trepidation, the wine-grower had returned home. Wife and children outdid themselves looking after his needs. They took off his well-worn clothes, washed his wounds and prepared a clean bed so he could rest comfortably.

The next morning, the long-suffering family patriarch still looked weak and bruised, but his friends and neighbors could not wait for him to tell them what had happened that fateful night so many years ago. In the hushed silence, the shaky voice told of past ordeals. That unforgettable night, pirates had surprised the wine-grower. He had been hopelessly outnumbered, bound and taken aboard the pirate vessel. Helplessly, he had watched as the wild sailors stole all of his grapes, ransacked the vineyard and then destroyed the chapel of Nossa Senhora dos Prazeres, even burning the wooden figure of the Virgin Mary.

At first, the pirates tried to force their prisoner to join their crew, but he refused. As punishment, he was thrown into a filthy dungeon in Morocco. However, the wine-grower did not manage to endure his tormentor's tortures for long and soon caved in and begged them to allow him to become a pirate on one of their raiding vessels.

One night, when the pirate ship he was on was gently swaying in the calm swell close to Santa Maria, the desolate Azorean decided to take fate into his own hands. He offered his fellow sailors to take the first watch, and while they peacefully snored under the twinkling stars, their unwilling co-pirate quietly hopped into a tub that had once been filled with whale blubber, and with the help of two oars, escaped his captors without them noticing anything until it was too late.

During his long years of captivity, the wine-grower had promised that if ever he were permitted to return to his native island, he would go barefoot all over Santa Maria on a pilgrimage asking for money to rebuild the chapel and buy a new statue of the Virgin Mary. As soon as the long-lost son of the island felt strong enough, he set off. At the completion of his promise, the family organized a sumptuous meal for all neighbors because the wine-grower was eternally grateful that he had been allowed to return home and live to a ripe old age amidst family and friends on his beloved island of Santa Maria.

"Bey, Bey"

It was especially in the 16th century that the Azoreans lived in constant fear of being attacked by pirates. Due to their geographic isolation and small numbers of inhabitants, the little islands in the northwestern and southeastern extremities of the Azorean archipelago were particularly prone to suffer from these hostile invasions.

Santa Maria, the smaller of the two southeastern islands, often found itself to be the first target for the corsairs on their route from northern Africa. After the collapse of the Ottoman Empire, tribal groups developed independently governed societies along the southern Mediterranean coast. Their commanders were called Bey and specialized in piracy. On their raids all the way up to Iceland, they kidnapped unsuspecting inhabitants and then either sold them as slaves in northern Africa or traded them back for ransom money.

In this way, the population of Santa Maria was depleted on various occasions. At one time, the pirates had the audacity to leave less than half the population behind. Fortunately, most of the inhabitants managed to return to their native island, although only after several months and arduous negotiations through societies in Lisbon specialized in these exchanges. Apart from looting for riches and ransacking, the wild sailors were also craving for food in order to replenish their ship rations. Consequently, the inhabitants of Santa Maria did not only mourn their kidnapped kinfolk, but also faced general devastation of their settlement.

Needless to say, the development of an effective warning system was foremost on their minds. As soon as an unfamiliar ship was spotted by the men at the look-out positions, they blew into their sea shell horns and shouted at the top of their voices: "The bey is coming! The bey is coming!" The islanders learned to gather their precious belongings in no time and rush to secluded caves and ravines, where they desperately hoped to avoid being found by the marauders.

The beys and their crews came and then they left again. Yet, the horror of that time lives on in numerous stories and legends. To this day, the word "bey" is still used in Santa Maria as an exclamation of awe and fear.

When, in long winter nights, the untameable Atlantic storms cause the waves to climb the shores of the battered island, and the ruthless winds try to sweep everything into the churning waters, the inhabitants huddle together for comfort around their warming fireplaces. Intimidated by the wrath of nature, they mutter in subdued voices: "Bey! Bey! Bey!" However, even on a brilliant summer day, the visitor who carelessly exposes his tender skin to the ever so cooling sea breeze, might seek redeeming help from the island's pharmacist. He will hand over the alleviating cream with a bewildered smile on his face and an astonished "Bey, bey, bey" mumbled under his breath.

The undeserved supper

A long time ago, a poor couple lived with their three sons in Vila do Porto on the Azorean island of Santa Maria. Their little house had a thatched roof and was right next to the church on the street that is nowadays called Rua António Coelho.

They led a very secluded life, and their only source of income was fishing. Although they never disturbed their neighbors, the neighbors did not approve of the poor family's disrespect for Sundays and holidays, in general. They were concerned and appalled to watch the parents and their children stubbornly go out to fish from dawn to dusk every single day of the week without ever attending mass.

One day, during the season of Lent, the neighbours agreed to invite the family to participate at least in the Easter festivities. However, one of the three sons haughtily turned on them and chided: "Do you think we have time to waste like you? You should well know that resting your lazy butt in the pews never filled anybody's stomach."

Slightly embarrassed, the neighbors withdrew and decided not to bother the embittered family again. They merely watched as the family spent even their scant days of relaxation looking for limpets at the seashore.

However, when on Maundy Thursday the family was traipsing towards the shore with their wicker baskets swinging in their hands, obviously intent on adding some variety to their supper that day by collecting limpets, their neighbors grew concerned, and they could hardly refrain from interfering. Call it faith or superstition, but no Azorean fisherman would ever go close to the coast on Maundy Thursday.

That Maundy Thursday morning, low tide found the water receding all the way down to the foot of the cliff. Lithely, the five limpet collectors were lured by the tasty crustaceans all the way down to the edge of the water. Of course, the father looked up to watch the shearwater return to their nests in the cliff, long before their usual time of the day. He understood this to be a sure sign of a storm to be raging over the open ocean. Yet, the sea seemed calm and quiet, and soon the whole family was absorbed collecting limpets.

They never noticed the long waves racing up to the coast from afar. Nobody was around to warn them. When they heard the rush of the water, it was already too late. Mercilessly, the very first wave pulled the family of five into the open sea. Nobody heard their desperate shouts, nobody saw their frantic gestures.

When, just before dusk, the parishioners returned from mass, they saw no light in the thatched-roof house. Fearing the worst, they rushed to the edge of the cliff. The sun was about to dip into the splendidly colored ocean. Right in front of the fiery disk, five objects floated in the distance. The people of Vila do Porto instantly assumed them to be the bodies of the missing family. After all, without honoring the day of the Lord, did they deserve supper anyhow? It was a lesson for everyone to learn, and that part of the coast became known as Ponta da Malmerenda, place of the undeserved supper.

The Cave of the Holy Christ

One cool morning in early autumn, an old woman from Vila do Porto on the Azorean island of Santa Maria went to the beach near Calhau do Peixe to collect firewood. She regularly used to do that because the sea always provided all kinds of flotsam and sometimes fishermen left behind scraps of wood, after having repaired one of their boats.

On returning home, the woman immediately went to kindle the fire in her stove with the odd pieces she had found. She was eager to take off the chill in the Atlantic humidity creeping into her house with the approaching winter months. With a sigh of content, she was just about to settle down comfortably, when one of the pieces of wood started to crackle and then fell out of the open fireplace as soon as the flames started to lick at it. She put it back three times, but each time the wood rolled out of the fire again before it could get scorched.

Surprised, the old woman went to inspect the uneven plank, and turning it around on all sides, she concluded that it more of less resembled the shape of a small wooden arm. As she did not know what to do next, she rushed to the church and confronted the priest with her discovery.

Curiously enough, that very morning some fishermen had rung the priest out of his sleep, because they had found a crucifix with a Christ figure in one of the caves along the cliff, while they were fishing in the early morning hours. Straight away, the fisherman had taken the cross to the priest, lamenting that the Christ figure was missing one arm. When the priest now held up to the crucifix the piece of wood that the old woman had brought, it proved to be the missing arm of the Christ figure.

One has to keep in mind that at the beginning of the 18th century, religious influence exerted immense social pressure on ordinary life. Thus, the coincidental discovery of these two parts of the same crucifix was interpreted as a divine miracle, something sent straight from heaven. Solemnly, the congregation carried the crucifix to the church, the Igreja da Misericórdia. Years later, it was moved to the Church of Senhor dos Passos, where still today, one can clearly see that the left arm was glued separately to complete the Christ figure.

The cave where the crucifix was found became known as the Furna de Santo Crist, the Cave of the Holy Christ. Morays are still being caught there, but a crucifix has not been found again.

The mermaid from Praia

In the little village of Praia on Santa Maria, one of the two south-eastern islands of the Azorean archipelago, there lived a fisherman with his grown son in a small cottage close to the shore. On moon-lit nights, they used to sit outside and while gazing over the glittering waves, they could sometimes hear sweet melodies rising up to them. Curiosity made the young man ask where these seducing tunes originated from. His father's face became serious as he warned his son that the enchanting voices of the mermaids lured men into the depths of the ocean. Of course, from then on, the young fisherman could not help but dream about the sweet temptation pulling him to the water's edge.

One bright night, when the full moon made the ocean gleam like livid silver, the young fisherman resolutely defied his father's warning and slunk down to the beach where he carefully hid behind a large boulder. For hours he waited, the sweet melodies tantalizing him, but no mermaids were to be seen. Finally, he could not bear it any longer and he desperately implored: "Mermaids of my fate, do not torment me to death!"

No sooner had he uttered his yearning desire, when he saw delicate figures rising out of the livid water. While they slid onto the beach he realized that they were only half human, their bodies ending in a fishtail. Yet, the young fisherman was so dazzled by their beauty that he stood there totally transfixed. Never had he seen skin shimmering like white alabaster, the mermaids' long locks of striking red hair falling down over it. Besides, the mermaids were singing so sweetly and swaying so gracefully that the young man completely fell under their spell. He came running out from behind his boulder, trying to catch one. Instantly, the mermaids skittered away into the security of the ocean. Only one did not move fast enough and was actually caught by the young man.

To his consternation, he found her violently bursting into tears, begging him to set her free. The fisherman, however, was so enchanted by the mermaid that he again whispered an imploring incantation while fervently kissing her neck. To his utter delight, the fishtail suddenly started to fall off and he held a lovely young woman in his arms.

He hastened back home and wasted no time marrying her. Soon after, they moved to Almagreira, where the fisherman became the father of a happy bunch of children. They all took after their mother, and today her descendants live scattered all over the island of Santa Maria. When you go to Almagreira, the pretty young girls with their alabaster-white skin and ravaging red hair will give you a faint glimpse of how beautiful that mermaid must have been when the fisherman found her.

Wheat for an enchanted island

Many years ago, a ship laden with wheat was passing south of Santa Maria, when, all of a sudden, the sailors saw a noble horseman galloping up to them while barely touching the skipping waves. The hard-boiled mariners were left petrified and speechless, but the horseman merely reigned in his white horse and asked in a pleasant voice if they would allow him to buy some sacks of wheat from their cargo.

The captain of the ship was so flabbergasted that he confined himself to asking in an equally amiable tone where the wheat was supposed to be deposited. The mysterious stranger pointed to the sea and assured him that the barn was down below. Then he invited the dumbfounded ship's captain to mount the white horse behind him and ride with him to receive his payment.

Mesmerized, like in a dream, the captain did as he was told and instantly found himself in a beautiful city in the depths of the ocean. As a matter of fact, the anchor of his ship was resting in the well-kept churchyard. In amazement, he watched the wheat orderly flowing through channels straight into the open barn. The cavalier did not stop to look, and so the captain rushed to follow him into his sumptuous house, where they were greeted by the loveliest young lady the captain had ever seen. The gallant nobleman introduced her as his daughter and noticed that the rough sailor had instantly lost his heart to this adorable young woman.

In a challenging manner, the nobleman turned to the captain and presented him with a choice: "Sir, either you receive the money for the wheat and return to your ship, or you take this opportunity to marry my daughter. If you decide to marry her, the spell that was cast over our island so many years ago will be lifted and we will be set free."

There was no doubt about it, the captain had fallen in love, head over heels. Yet, at the same time, he did not forget his responsibility towards his crew and the delivery of the cargo. Resolutely, he answered: "My dearest wish is to wed your daughter, but first I have to deliver my ship with its cargo." Thus, he mounted the white horse and returned to his ship with the payment for the wheat.

Taking his responsibilities very seriously, the captain delivered his wheat as fast as possible, and then returned to the spot where he thought he had met the gallant horseman. He searched and searched, but could not find the enchanted island. For years to come, his voyages would take him to the area where he assumed the beautiful city to be, but he never found it again, and thus he never married the dazzling young lady that lived on in his heart.

Until this day, King Sebastiao's island remains on the bottom of the sea, waiting eternally for anyone to lift the spell that was cast so long ago.

Terceira

A story about Nossa Senhora do Livramento, Our Lady of Liberation

During one of those raids in which Muslim pirates haunted the Azores throughout the 16th and 17th centuries, a profoundly religious man was kidnapped from Terceira, which is an island in the central group of the Azorean archipelago. The man was particularly devoted to Nossa Senhora do Livramento, Our Lady of Liberation, but, of course, he could not express his Christian faith in Muslim slavery. He was taken to northern Africa, where all day long, he had to work very hard as a soldier.

At night, however, he often managed to sneak away and meet other Christian slaves. Together they prayed and celebrated the Christian holidays. One day, though, the Muslim commander found out about his slave's nightly excursions. The master became very furious and had his minion locked up in a big box to sleep in at night.

However, this confinement did not keep the Azorean devotee of Nossa Senhora do Livramento from skipping out of the box and joining his brethren in prayer. The slave owner became livid with rage. He ordered his Azorean slave not only to be locked up, but also to be guarded by a heavily armed sentinel who had to lie on top of the box, which was supposed to prevent an escape even if the guard succumbed to inevitable sleep. No one was more surprised than the sentinel when he awoke in the early hours with the slave praying in front of the locked box.

Nothing is known about the fate of the Azorean slave, but in the church of Nossa Senhora do Livramento, there used to be a sculpture of a soldier lying on a box with a kneeling Christian in front of it. Unfortunately, the church was completely destroyed during the earthquake of 1980, and the sculpture has never been seen again.

The legend of Santo Amaro in Ribeirinha

Many years ago, some men went to the coast to fish. They were from the fishing village of Ribeirinha on the Azorean island of Terceira. While they were casting out their bait and patiently waiting for fish to bite, they suddenly spotted a box rolling among the pebbles with the in-coming tide.

Curiosity got the better of them, and they pulled the box out and opened it. To their greatest amazement, inside they found a statue of Santo Amaro. Hastily they gathered their fishing gear together and carried the saint to the church.

The next day, as the delighted priest set about to read mass in front of the newly found figure, he realized that it was gone. The congregation was as perplexed as the priest, and they all spread out to look for the fugitive saint. Finally, somebody discovered it in a nook at the bottom of the cliff, close to the place where it had been found.

Triumphantly, the saint was carried back to the church, but the very next morning, it was found to have escaped this place of honor yet again. Some of the villagers claimed they had heard the statue clattering down the dry riverbed in the middle of the night. Tia Eugénia da Cruz, an elderly spinster who lived at the crossroads and could not even afford olive oil to light her house at night, had resorted to doing her spinning on her balcony, whenever the moonlight provided enough visibility. Night after night, Tia Eugénia watched the saint slip away from the church. She finally asked Santo Amaro why he did that instead of enjoying the company of the other venerable saints in the cool church building. Tia Eugénia claimed that, as an answer, the saint despondently shook his head and explained that the church was the house of the holy fisherman Peter. Saint Peter had eventually been made Pope, while he, Santo

Amaro, had only been a humble monk and, as that, would prefer to be venerated in a small chapel.

The congregation and their priest honored the saint's wish and built him a small chapel, where, still today, pilgrims leave their offerings on the day of Santo Amaro. He is said to have wrought many miracles, and faithful believers bring bread and Alfenim in the shape of body parts that have been cured or other objects representing wishes that came true.

By the way, Alfenim was developed as an artistic way of preserving sugar, because in former centuries, this costly food item would easily have melted or spoiled during its transport across the humid Atlantic Ocean. Adding a small quantity of vinegar allowed the Azoreans to create a stiff mass that hardened and remained preserved for quite some time. As sugar was precious, local artisans learned to mold it into a great variety of decorative shapes, which, even nowadays, can either be used as religious offerings, decorative presents or a treat for your sweet tooth. It also lends itself to being transported in suitcases via air travel and does not require special attention in your hand luggage.

The statue of the Jesus child of royal protection

It was one of those foggy afternoons in December, sometime at the end of the 16th century, when in the humid Azores, now and then much alike, dusk was about to settle into night. In the town of Praia on the island of Terceira, the nuns of the Order of Jesus were busy with their preparations of the Christmas festivities, when suddenly they heard the muffled sound of somebody knocking at the gates of their convent. Outside, there stood a little old woman who was offering a small Jesus statue in exchange for bread.

The nuns were delighted and invited the fragile woman to join them and partake in their opulent Christmas dinner. Afterwards, they led her to an unoccupied cell so that she could spend the night in comfortable warmth. Everybody slept contentedly until late morning, and then the nuns went to see whether the old woman had also enjoyed a good night's sleep. To their great amazement, they found the bed untouched, but covered with sweet smelling rose petals. Full of curiosity, the nuns asked around in the population if anybody knew the whereabouts of the old woman, but nobody had ever seen her around.

Thus, the nuns concluded that the frail beggar had been none other than the Virgin Mary herself, who had chosen to spend Christmas Eve with them, offering the small statue of Jesus as a present to the convent. Reverently, they carried the small statue to a chapel of its own. There it is said to have worked many miracles, notably those for the daughter of King Pedro II. She was born a frail infant suffering from all kinds of maladies. The royal family chose to mark her birthday, January 6, with joyous festivities that for years had the whole population of Terceira gather and join in.

Later, the small figure of Jesus was bedded in a delicately chiseled cradle of genuine silver and taken to the main church of Praia. Due to the high esteem in which the figure was held by the royal family, it became known as Menino Jesus da Real Proteccao, Jesus child of royal protection.

Mary and the sunny Saturdays on Terceira

On Terceira, the saying goes that there is no Saturday without sun, no Sunday without mass, and no Monday without laziness. Of course, a religious explanation is offered to justify this lifestyle.

Jesus's Mother Mary was poor and only had one outfit of clothes for her little son. Yet, she did not want him to go to church all soiled. So, on Saturday morning she quickly washed all clothes, and then prayed to the Lord for sunshine. God understood Mary's plight, as he still understands today the workload of mothers in

Terceira, and he made the sun shine with all its might so that the clothes were dry in no time.

This way, everybody can go to church in clean clothes on Sunday. On Monday, however, even little Jesus did not pay much attention to his garments while playing, and soon they would look grimy again. Which shows that Jesus is a tangible figure – while the Holy Spirit is revered as the central religious deity.

The hermitage of Nossa Senhora dos Milagres, in Serreta

At the end of the 16th century, there lived on the Azorean island of Terceira an elderly priest who became bitterly disappointed by some inexplicable injustice. He decided to withdraw from the company of his fellow human beings and from worldly life in general. He picked a pilgrim's staff and a small statue of the Virgin Mary and roamed the island until he found a secluded spot at the most westerly tip of the island that served his Spartan needs.

All by himself, he built a humble hermitage to shelter him and the small statue. He contented himself by surviving on the scarce food provided in nature, and he spent his days praying at the feet of the little Madonna, thus, in his solitude, finding peace of mind.

After the priest's death, the little hermitage soon fell into decay, and a new one was erected some distance away. It attracted many pilgrims, but among them were some who desecrated the holy shrine, and, therefore, the statue of the Virgin Mary had to be transferred to the dignified village church of Doze Ribeiras. There it is said to have worked numerous miracles, so that, eventually, a brotherhood called *Escravos da Senhora*, Slaves of Our Lady, was founded. The brotherhood then had the original hermitage rebuilt, providing the statue with a dignified home.

Today the statue is known as Nossa Senhora dos Milagres and enjoys its place of honor in the village church of Serreta. Each year, at the beginning of September, the inhabitants are joined by friends from the neighboring islands and walk to the church in a pilgrimage that increasingly attracts the whole population. Endurance and fitness seem to be as much on display as are religious conviction and devout suffering. At every corner, the Red Cross awaits tired walkers who miscalculated the comfort of their footwear and yearn to get their sore feet covered with soothing creams and bandages. The skillful villagers offer traditional home-made delicacies from open doors and windows. In Serreta the church door is wide open, welcoming the weary traveler. From across the street, the enticing smell of freshly baked bread with spicy sausage never fails to attract throngs of customers – despite the variety of treats tasted along the path of the pilgrimage: corn on the cob, muffins, melons, ice-cream ... No time for dieting, however frugal the monk might once have lived.

The legend of the little sea devils

It was the night of October 28, which for the Catholic Church is the day of Saint Simon and Saint Judas. In the middle of the north Atlantic, the inhabitants of the Azorean island of Terceira know that this is a particularly good night for sea devils to come ashore. That night, the islanders never fail to eat garlic and make sure they draw a cross with a clove of garlic on the entrance door and afterwards waste no time locking themselves behind closed doors and windows. No fisherman would dream of going out to sea that night. From experience, the inhabitants of Terceira know that the sea devils conjure gale-force winds and high waves and spur them on until these natural forces threaten to devour the land and leave nobody spared. Everybody in Terceira remembers that these infernal demons choose to play their wildest games of destruction on the nights of October 28 and February 2. In general, the inhabitants of Terceira wisely exercise caution on these nights of unpredictable danger.

So it was either sheer necessity or plain stubbornness that once made one fisherman decide to brave the elements and go fishing and defy all superstition. Of course, he could not find anyone to accompany him. As a precaution, he ate his share of garlic and hung the rest of a clove around his neck. Then he set off to the harbor, where he swiftly proceeded to push his boat into the swirling waters and headed straight out into the open sea.

However, he soon found out that not much could be done with regard to fishing. The fisherman started to feel uncomfortable and regretted his rash decision. There he was, engulfed in the pitch-dark fury of the night, with unruly high waves crashing and thundering against the creaking boat planks.

Suddenly, very clearly and distinctly, the fisherman could hear a voice right behind him: "What are you waiting for? Don't you want to throw this man into the sea?" The fisherman cowered down in panic as a second voice answered despondently: "Well, I wish I could, but unfortunately the man ate garlic, and he even slung some cloves around his neck, too."

There was no doubt left in the fisherman's mind: two sea devils were obviously discussing his fate. As fast as he could, the man rowed back to shore, vowing that he would never again get close to the sea on any one of those fateful nights. Meekly, he had to admit that the old adage was a warning that should best be followed: "On the day of Saint Simon lock your boats behind gates." At this time of the year, the weather conditions normally have set their minds to prove that this warning is nothing but an appeal to common sense. It just stands to reason!

How the fishing village Porto Judeu got its name

At the time of the first large-scale settlements in Terceira, about 500 years ago, a Portuguese caravel approached the island with its sailors scrutinizing the coastline in order to find a suitable place to set ashore. At last, they spotted a bay which was obviously well-suited as a natural harbor. The process of disembarking began, but it proved to be complicated while the rolling waves heaved the little boats up and down, up and down. As much as the passengers were filled with the anticipation of putting their feet on firm ground again, they first had to pluck up all of their courage to jump ashore, one after the other.

One Jewish settler got so scared by the waves splashing up to pull him into their cold grasp that he could not move at all. Petrified, he stared onto the rolling tide and kept everybody behind him waiting. Finally, one of the bawdy sailors lost his patience and roared: "Hey, Jew, either you jump, or I jump! Make up your mind!" The hesitant man seemed to snap out of a trance. In desperation, he closed his eyes and screamed: "I will jump, and the harbor will be mine."

Several people sneered and laughed, but the Jew jumped, found steady footing, and the disembarking could continue. The settlers grasped the fortunate opportunity and built a nice harbor at this convenient place. It did not take long until their first houses became part of a vibrant fishing village. Amidst guffaws and laughter, the episode of the Jew's disembarking was told so often that everybody finally referred to the new settlement as Porto do Judeu, Harbor of the Jew. The Jewish passenger, arriving amongst that first group of residents, never actually owned either the harbor or the village. In the end, he received the honor of owning the place, as we still know it today, in name only.

The tragedy of Má Marenda on Terceira

At the beginning of the 16th century, there lived a nobleman on the Azorean island of Terceira, whose name is better forgotten. He had a lovely daughter who fell head over heels in love with a young farm worker, while her father was busy arranging for her a convenient marriage with an old nobleman.

The young farmhand decided to go to sea to make his fortune in order to gain some credibility in the eyes of his prospective father-in-law. In the meantime, the nobleman wanted to take advantage of the young suitor's absence and tried to force his daughter to accept the arranged marriage. However, the girl steadfastly refused and infuriated her father so much with her stubbornness that he had her imprisoned in a small fort on the promontory in Praia. In order to break her will, the hard-hearted nobleman put his daughter on a Spartan diet of bread and water.

The delicate young girl of noble upbringing did not fare well in these harsh conditions and soon contracted an incurable disease. On her deathbed, she asked to be buried where she had spent her last days of suffering. No sooner was her wish granted, than the young sailor returned with his small fortune. When he learned of his beloved's death, he broke down, gave all his worldly possessions to the poor and needy and became a monk.

However, he did not survive for long either. His heart had been broken, the meagre rations in the damp monastery made him fall seriously ill and he, too, died. His last wish was to be buried right next to the young noblewoman he had loved so much.

On cold winter days, when the ocean is raging around the place where the two lovers chose to be united forever, one clearly hears them lamenting loudly about their tragic destiny. But on mild summer days, when one enjoys the sunshine on the idyllic promontory of Má Marenda, the sparse supper, the two unfortunate souls keep whispering in one another's ears, and their moaning is filled with infinite melancholy.

The legend of the Lagoa do Negro

At the time of the burgeoning settlements in the Azorean islands, Portugal was keen to preserve its dominance in the profitable Atlantic slave trade. Needless to say, the noble families of that time could not imagine how to maintain their estates without a respectable number of slaves.

Once, the only daughter of one of Terceira's noble families was made to enter one of those arranged marriages whose only objective was to increase the family fortune and secure a respected continuation of the lineage. Nobody ever thought about asking the girl for her personal opinion on the subject. Nor did anybody care to contemplate whether she would be happy or desolate in this union. The girl, being brought up in these traditional circumstances, surrendered to her fate and submitted herself to her husband´s orders without ever raising her voice once.

At that time, not even members of the nobility were entitled to act on their personal preferences, and slaves were not even regarded as human beings. Slaves were therefore thought to be lacking sentiments and feelings altogether. However, nature proved to be stronger than human foible and, unexpectedly, took its course.

The unassuming young noblewoman and a socially non-existent slave discovered a glowing passion for one another that caught both of them off their guard. Some afternoons, the young lady could be seen strolling through the garden of the manor, singing the sweetest love songs. On other occasions, her heart would wrench in dismay because she was well aware of the hopelessness of her forbidden love. Tears would stream down her cheeks and soak the delicate linen embroidery she was working on.

The slave saw his beloved mistress suffer and he knew that there was no hope for either of them. Inevitably, one of the house servants discovered the lovers' secret, and she went straight to her master to denounce his wife. The slave, meanwhile, had come to the sad conclusion that he could no longer bear to watch his beloved suffer without the slightest hope of a happy union. As he well realized, they would never be given a chance to be together, and so he painfully decided to run away and leave the island to end all wretchedness.

No sooner had he set off, when he heard his master's men following him on horseback, their dogs yapping in hot pursuit. He ran as fast as he could, climbing into the inaccessible interior of the island. Finally, he sank to his knees, depleted of all energy. In the distance, he heard the horsemen and dogs drawing closer in spite of the difficult terrain. He knew there was no escaping his fate, and tears started to well out of his eyes, forming a small lake. When the first horsemen came scrambling over the last crest, the unfortunate slave threw himself into the water in front of him and drowned.

Today the serene landscape surrounding the unruffled waters evokes an unforgettable picture of peaceful beauty. However, the lake will forever remind the people of Terceira of the tragic love between a slave and a noble lady.

Heduvige´s dream

On the Azorean island of Terceira, there lived a charming young girl called Heduvige, whose shimmering blond hair and sparkling blue eyes bedazzled every man who gazed upon her. Her father was a successful merchant from Flanders, whom King Sebastiao had entrusted with the monopoly of trading the rare dyeing plants urzela, a lichen, and pastel, called woad, that grew in the Azores and were much sought after in the English textile industry in the 16th century. In addition to that, Heduvige's father was overseeing the commerce in spices coming from India, like cloves, pepper and cinnamon, which means that the family could afford to lead a comfortable lifestyle.

Therefore, Heduvige could have enjoyed a learned education in the prestigious convent of Esperanca, but she chose to complete her education with her uncle Zózimo, who had been studying in Florence, Italy, to become an accomplished painter. The young artist entertained his adoring niece with stories about his knowledge of reading the future and turned her interest to the abounding diversity of blooming flowers.

One day, Heduvige sought her uncle's advice, distress disturbing her pretty face. She did not know what to make of a nightmare that had spoiled her good night's sleep. She had dreamt that she was walking through a gloomy forest of weeping willows next to a rushing river overflowing with the tears of utter despair. Then, quite unexpectedly, she had found herself in a bright grove of light-green willows, whose fluffy yellow catkins bobbed above a happily babbling brook, where a handsome young man was waiting, smiling expectantly at her.

At that point, Heduvige was awakened by the untimely crowing of the estate's rooster. Imploringly, she now turned her confused eyes to her uncle Zózimo, who soothingly took her hands into his and explained the dream to her. There were days lying ahead, full of worry and distress, but they would be followed by times of joy and consoling happiness.

Although Heduvige was left reassured, she was curious and pondered what life held in store for her. Restlessly, she tossed around in her bed the following night, when the moon made the sea glitter like livid silver, while the soothing August breeze gently caressed the five central islands of the Azorean archipelago. Suddenly, a piercing scream echoed through the peaceful night: "Pirates! Pirates!" From her window, the bewildered girl watched as her father and some slaves were bound and then taken away by fierce looking villains, while her beloved uncle Zózimo collapsed in a pool of blood after being struck down with a gleaming dagger in the hands of a ruthless outlaw.

The wild sailors robbed and looted, and after they had filled their ship with food and treasures, they took Heduvige and sailed away. When the sun rose out of the eastern ocean, close to the island of São Miguel, a heavily armed Spanish merchant ship slipped out of the shadow of the awakening island and headed straight up to the pirate ship. A fierce battle ensued, and Heduvige fell onto her knees in prayer, tears streaming down her face.

Soon, the pirates were overwhelmed, and the Spaniards boarded the ship. The young captain, Nicolau, found Heduvige cowering in a corner, desperate and frightened. Respectfully, he addressed her and explained that she was to fear no more. Once he had gained her confidence, Nicolau could not help but fall in love with the beautiful young woman. Heduvige calmed down and, to her great astonishment, recognized Nicolau as the charming young man from her bewildering dream.

Nicolau's ship took them safely back home, and the following April, Andalusia witnessed the most splendid marriage of Heduvige and Nicolau. They named their first son Zózimo, because dreams do not lie and show us the path into the future, if only we believe in them.

Graciosa

A father's promise

It was in the year 1669, and night fell on Graciosa, the smallest island of the Azorean central group. The family of the town provost, Gil de Quadros, was sitting comfortably in their living room, having just finished their evening prayers. Gil de Quadros was an imposing man, bearing his family name with pride, and he was complacently reminiscing about the heroic counterattack that his father had led against marauding pirates in 1629. Quite unexpectedly, a skittish bat chose this very moment of tranquillity and repose to come flying through the open window and give the house servants a hard time as they desperately tried to shoo the little intruder out.

A chill had settled over the provost's family, and, feeling uncomfortable, they dispersed and went to bed. After a night of bad dreams, undoubtedly caused by the tales of superstition and by the bad luck omens evoked by the mysterious appearance of the little bat, they were all awakened early by a messenger from Vila da Praia, urgently knocking on the front door. English pirates had used the darkness of the night to ransack the unsuspecting town on the other side of the island.

At once, the town provost sounded the general alarm and organized the defense system of Santa Cruz. While busying himself this way, he also took some time to pray for heavenly protection, in the course of which he promised that if the town were to be spared from a devastating attack, he would send his two young daughters, Clélia and Anunciação, to a convent.

In the meantime, the pirates had successfully looted Vila da Praia and abundantly replenished their ship's rations. Contentedly, they set off to look for more treasures in the neighboring islands. Thus, Vila de Santa Cruz had escaped their attention, and the provost's daughters came to learn what their father had decided for their lives. The two girls cried their eyes out, but although it nearly broke their father's heart, the man stood firm and shipped his desperate daughters to the neighboring island of Terceira, where the gates of the Capuchin convent closed behind them.

Clélia fatalistically submitted to the convent's routine, but Anunciacão rebelled and steadfastly refused to adapt. One of their aunts happened to be the abbess of the convent and was filled with pity for the two young sisters. She wrote long letters to her brother imploring him to reconsider his position, but her brother refused and insisted on honoring his promise, while, at the same time, his conscience never allowed him to find peace.

On Good Friday, Gil de Quadros was still plagued by this state of inner turmoil. He desolately prayed at the feet of the statue of Nossa Senhora da Ajuda, when, suddenly, he heard a soft voice advising him: "If on the day of Ascension you see two immaculately white doves rise from the cross at Porto da Barra, the Lord will release you from your promise because of your faithfulness."

Hardly could Gil de Quadros wait for that Holy Thursday to come. As soon as light broke, he was kneeling in front of the cross. Two immaculately white doves rose and flew up into the early morning sunlight. The relieved father wasted no time and sailed to Terceira that very morning. His daughters were overjoyed to be allowed to return home and proceeded with their worldly lives until they peacefully died of old age surrounded by their adoring children and grandchildren.

The corsair and the cross made of solid gold

In the 15th century, the Azorean island of Graciosa suffered enumerable pirate attacks. The pirates looted, torched, destroyed and killed whatever they could lay their hands on. Small wonder, the survivors did not harbor any kind feelings for these rampaging attackers. Consequently, not too many pirates chose this island to turn their lives around.

However, one French pirate, called Laplace, ended up staying behind because he lost his heart to an innocent young maiden with gentle eyes and ravaging dark curls. The first time he saw her, she was on her way to church. His heart gave a leap, and although she hastily averted her gaze, he detected her cheeks blushing conspicuously. It was love at first sight, and soon the girl revealed that she was ready to return his feelings.

As one can imagine, the girl's parents were not amused by these unexpected developments. They went to great lengths in order to dissuade their daughter from seeing her unacceptable suitor. They went as far as to forbid her to attend Holy Mass so that the devil, whom in their eyes the uncouth corsair impersonated, would not get a chance to lead her into temptation. They wasted no time in searching high and low for a respectable man worthy of their daughter. To their great dismay, they found out that these men were either already married or they were engaged and could not be pried out of their commitments.

At this point, the once obedient daughter discovered her trait of Azorean stubbornness. Vehemently, she declared that she would only marry the man she truly loved and that she had set her mind on marrying Laplace.

The pirate was impressed by the girl's courage, for confronting her parents and risking her reputation in the small village community. From his hidden treasure trove, he carefully picked a cross of solid gold studded with sparkling gems, and sent it to his prospective father-in-law.

The girl's father instantly understood the message and was relieved to find out that the pirate was wealthy enough to support a comfortable lifestyle for his daughter, and understood that the golden cross had indeed been offered as an olive branch, through which the lawless pirate professed to be of Christian faith. As no further objections were raised, the marriage preparations joyfully commenced, and soon after, the once wild pirate and the once humble village maiden were pronounced husband and wife and lived happily ever after.

The hot springs of Carapacho

A few centuries ago, a farmer in Carapacho on the small Azorean island of Graciosa made a comfortable living keeping two or three cows on the side. One day, his strongest cow lost her appetite, her shanks started sagging, and, day after day, she grew skinnier.

Fervently, the farmer and his wife busied themselves administering all the remedies they had ever heard of. The cow was made to drink camomile tea, was rubbed with an evil smelling tincture a neighbor gave them, was made to inhale the medicinal fumes that had once helped the ailing grandmother, and, finally, the desperate couple even approached a faith-healer. Yet, nothing worked, and the cow was already reduced to skin and bones, so much so that the children were horrified at the sight of it.

With a deep sigh of regret, the farmer decided to walk the cow to the Ponta de Restinga, where it would either succumb to its weakness or be slaughtered for its sparse meat rations, if its owner plucked up his courage for this final act of mercy. Slowly, the cow trotted ahead of the farmer who prodded her with a stick to keep her going. When they passed a little well gurgling cheerfully at the side of their path, the cow hesitated for a moment and then bent down to quench its thirst.

To his greatest surprise, the farmer observed an almost instant change in the cow's demeanor. The cow's eyes started to sparkle again, and her rough coat suddenly looked smooth again. Excitedly, the farmer let the recovering animal drink to its heart's content. Then they turned around and plodded home.

Every day the family members took turns supplying the cow with fresh drinking water from the very well they had accidentally stumbled across. Soon, word spread, and humans and animals alike came to drink the medicinal water in order to miraculously cure all kinds of ailments.

The thermal hot springs of Carapacho became famous, until, eventually, they drifted into oblivion. Today, the well's curative properties are again being sought. But whether you suffer from rheumatism or not, spending a day in the mild breeze of the tranquil bay of Carapacho will always refresh your body and soul and remain in your memory as the perfect Azorean harmony between humankind and nature.

The cave of Maria Encantada

Many years ago, a well-to-do couple lived at the bottom of a lovely valley on the Azorean island of Graciosa. As was customary at that time, they owned a variety of domestic animals, all joining in a happy cacophony that underlined the lively spirit of that idyllic place.

One night, at a rather untimely hour, the wife, called Maria, heard the cock crow in a strangely shrill voice. For three consecutive days, it kept repeating this agitated shrieking, and Maria nervously claimed she could hear a warning: "Flee now! Flee now! Before it is too late." Her husband told her to be quiet and not make a spectacle of herself. With scorn in his voice, he laughed in her face and declared that he would never desert his extensive property and that his wife should not go anywhere either.

Not many days later, the ground began to shake and rumble. Then, the peaceful valley burst open and red-hot lava gushed out, devouring the well-kept property together with its unlucky owners, leaving just a gaping cave behind.

Since then, the chided housewife Maria has regularly been spotted on a hill called Facho that sits on the rugged ridge surrounding the crater where the farm once stood. She and her three daughters, Rosa, Maria and Madalena, live their enchanted lives tending their livestock. Now and again, somebody claims to spot her clad in rags, chasing barking dogs away from her flock of sheep. In Fenais, everybody knows that the seagulls shrieking above one's head are actually Maria's enchanted chicken. Now and again, the local urchins try to annoy her. They creep up to the edge of the menacing hole in the ground and hurl stones down into it. Afterwards, they maintain that they clearly discerned the sound of broken china coming all the way up from the abyss. On calm summer days, Maria´s white linen is said to be drying above the opening of the caldera, shimmering in the reassuring sunlight.

If you are bold enough, you can still go into the cave of the enchanted Maria by taking the Canada da Furna and turning right at the path that leads down to the crater. There you will be surprised to see the remains of her spade and sieve marked in the cave´s ceiling.

The mermaid and the fisherman

Many years ago, when a fisherman walked along a beach of Graciosa, the smallest island of the Azorean central group, as he often used to do, he quite unexpectedly jolted in midstride. Somebody was bitterly sobbing close by although he could not see anyone. Carefully, he peered over a rugged boulder dripping with wet algae that had been left high and dry by the receding tide. He could hardly believe his eyes – a delicate mermaid was sitting there crying her eyes out.

Well, every fisherman knows that one should never trust a mermaid, if one does not want to be pulled to the bottom of the ocean without returning to land ever again. Therefore, the young fisher-

man made sure to keep his distance when he stepped out from behind the boulder, but he was curious to find out why the delicate
mermaid was gripped by such sadness. At the sight of him, she
became so frightened that she stopped sobbing and started to tremble all over. She explained that she had been stranded by this boulder because she had not paid any attention to the water leaving the
bay, and now she could not reach the ocean. Dejectedly, she
pointed at her shimmering fishtail. Pleadingly, she raised her eyes,
still overflowing with tears, up to the young man and shyly asked
if he would be so kind as to carry her back to the water.

Again, the fisherman was on his guard, and hastily stepped back.
Then another thought crossed his mind. However apprehensive he
was about approaching the unpredictable ocean with a mermaid in
his arms, there always had been one wish he had not known how
to fulfill. Bravely, he faced the fragile mermaid and told her that,
if he returned her to the water, he wanted her to bring him one of
those stones that came crashing down to earth from out of the sky
– or was it heaven? – and that were now lying on the bottom of the
sea.

The mermaid nodded her head in agreement, but asked one favor
in return. She wanted to take a sack of broad beans back down to

her underwater kingdom. The deal was agreed upon, and the fisherman picked up the slippery mermaid in his arms, making sure not to drop her, and carried her to the water. Lithely, she dove into the welcoming waves, and the fisherman turned to fetch his sack of broad beans from home.

On his return, he did not have to wait long. The mermaid's head reappeared, bobbing between the dancing waves. Deftly, she threw the stone onto the beach, and the fisherman tossed the sack of broad beans in her direction. With a smile on her lips, the mermaid waved to the fisherman and vanished in the ocean.

The young man carefully scrutinized the rare stone from all sides. His long-held wish had been fulfilled. Many times, he returned to the spot where he had once found the sobbing mermaid, but he never saw another one in his entire life. But that doesn't mean the unsuspecting tourist might not stumble over one. Have you tried?

São Jorge

The Holy-Spirit-cattle of Topo

In São Jorge, as in all the other Azorean islands, belief in the Holy Spirit determines everybody's lives, finding its ultimate communal expression in the Holy-Spirit-festivities around Whit Sunday. In the morning, every passer-by is offered bread and milk, and at lunchtime, everybody is invited to partake in a sumptuous festive meal consisting of the traditional Holy-Spirit-soup, meat in all its variations and, at some places, sweet rice with cinnamon. Of course, you are encouraged to drink the local wine to accompany this banquet.

One year, the organizer of the Holy-Spirit-festivities, called _mordomo_, had promised to feed the whole population of Topo. Therefore, he had taken two oxen to the little verdant islets separated from the main island by no more than a few hundred meters. In order to take cattle to these lush pastures, one leads them behind a little boat, ropes keeping their heads high out of the water.

The month of May came, and quite uncharacteristically, rough winds and high waves continued to take the Azoreans' breath away. The *mordomo* cast a worried look onto the lush pastures on the little islets where his oxen were growing fatter and fatter, but from where it was impossible to retrieve them in this kind of weather. At the last minute, the *mordomo* felt compelled to buy yet two other oxen in order to keep his promise and feed the inhabitants of Topo on Whit Sunday. Although he did not feel comfortable about this transaction, because these were not the same oxen that he had promised, he felt certain that the Holy Spirit would understand.

On Friday morning, the *mordomo* and his neighbors and friends set to work and slaughtered the newly-bought oxen. No sooner were they cutting up the different parts of the meat, when, to the amazement of everyone present, the two oxen that were initially promised to the Holy Spirit came calmly treading up to the scene. Nobody understood how they had managed to swim to the island without assistance, and, besides, they were not wet, as would have been expected.

The people looked at one another and came to the conclusion that the Holy Spirit must have carried them across the water to help the *mordomo* keep his promise. With tears in his eyes, the owner of the oxen all too happily agreed to slaughter them, in addition to the two other ones. Never had Topo seen more opulent festivities than in that joyful year.

Why one should respect the Holy Spirit

Some time ago in Topo on the Azorean island of São Jorge, there lived a young and quite happily married couple. However, the years passed by without their dearest wish, that of conceiving a baby, ever coming true. Finally, they became convinced that their prayers had not been answered because of former sins or lack of charitable assistance. Therefore, they promised they would provide for the Holy-Spirit-feast on Whit Sunday, if the wife were to expect a child.

Not long after having made this promise, the woman became pregnant, and the couple started looking for a meat source as a mainstay of the Holy-Spirit-banquet. The husband finally obtained a suitable bull from a farmer who kept his cattle grazing in the interior of the island, where he needed to check on them only sporadically. One needs to know that Azorean cows are happy cows that spend their entire lives grazing on lush green pastures in the open air and are never confined to stifling stables. Even in the less hospitable winter season, the temperatures seldom dip below zero degrees Celsius/32 degrees Fahrenheit.

Contentedly, the expectant father tied the bull in his barn and went about finishing his daily chores, humming after having accomplished that part of his promise. When he returned in the evening to check on his new acquisition, he was by no means prepared for what he found in the stable. The bull had become frightened by the sudden confinement in an unaccustomed environment and had broken loose trying to escape. In that process, the interior of the barn had been destroyed to such an extent that, when the bull's new owner saw the chaos, he became blind with rage, grasped the nearest tool at hand and started bearing down with a scythe on the panicking sacrifice to the Holy Spirit.

Attracted by the noise in the barn, the pregnant wife came rushing out of the house and saw her husband mistreating the suffering animal. She threw herself in his arms and implored him to stop. Her husband, however, was still heaving with anger and heatedly replied: "Why do you care? It does not matter. The bull will be sacrificed to the Holy Spirit anyway, and it has already been paid for."

As it was, the Holy-Spirit-feast on Whit Sunday turned out to be to everybody's liking, and all the neighbors and friends wished the couple well. The woman carried her baby to term, and, in due time, gave birth to a healthy little girl. However, to her parents' grief, the child's face bore the marks of the welts that the bull for the

Holy Spirit had suffered at the hands of her father. Out of shame, the couple raised their child hidden in their house, and even as an adult, she never dared leave the house without a shawl or veil covering her face.

Everybody knew that her disfigurement was the Holy Spirit's punishment for her father's lack of respect. This legend explains the plight of children with special needs or handicaps who, until quite recently, were kept hidden at home out of the underlying assumption that the disfigurement was a punishing sign from the Holy Spirit. The development of the Azorean archipelago amidst European integration opened new perspectives, relocated the islands in an international context – and established the acceptance of citizens with special needs.

The legend of Vela Latina

On May 1, 1808, a strong earthquake shook the Azorean island of São Jorge, and at Lagoinhas, close to Urzelina, an angry volcano erupted. A mighty stream of glowing lava poured down to the coast and covered everything in its path, pastures, fields and houses. Disoriented, people fled in all directions to escape the general mayhem, while the devastating destruction did not spare the village of Urzelina and covered it with a thick layer of molten stone.

When, after days of fear and chaos, the volcano stopped spewing and the soil cooled down, the inhabitants returned to face the transformed landscape. To their utter amazement, they found a herd of cattle, dedicated to the Holy Spirit, miraculously unharmed and untouched, the cows grazing on a triangular pasture as if nothing had happened. Even today, one can clearly see in the present eucalyptus grove where the lava stream once split, sparing the offering to the Holy Spirit.

The legend about the Canada do Inferno, the "Path to Hell"

Many years ago, a very rich man lived in the village of Ribeira Seca. All over the Azorean island of São Jorge, he was held in high esteem and everybody treated him reverently, reading his lips as if he were the king himself. However, one day, he was summoned to court in Velas to give testimony about an alleged homicide.

On the day of the trial, he mounted his horse, but the closer he got to Velas, the more he disliked the notion of being treated just like any other ordinary person before the law. Gradually, he developed a fiendish plan to free himself of this predicament. During the trial, he unscrupulously committed perjury and implicated a poor neighbor, who, of course, proved to be no match for the highly honored lord of a manor and was subsequently sentenced. With a smirk on his face, the undeserving culprit mounted his horse because he wanted to return home as fast as possible in order to celebrate his shrewdness.

Night had already fallen when all of a sudden, a glowing stream of fire blocked his path in the pitch darkness. Sparks flew in all directions, the ground hissed and smoke billowed up to the thin-sliced moon. Petrified, the rich man repented of his despicable behavior. His guilty conscience prevailed, and he promised to ride back to Velas and recant, if the Virgin Mary saved him from being swallowed by the fires of hell. On bent knees, he observed how the fiery flow came to a halt and cooled down, allowing him to return to Velas. Shamefacedly, he admitted to his wrongdoings. The perjury sentence was revoked, the poor neighbor acquitted and amply rewarded. Justice was done with regards to the homicide, and the perjurious man saw his reputation and riches greatly diminished.

Out of gratitude for having his prayers answered when he was facing hell's burning fires, the humbled man even had a chapel built in honor of the Virgin Mary. The road he took that led him to repent the false judgement is still called Canada do Inferno, the path to hell. – Or the positive educational effects of unforeseeable natural disasters. Ethics, thanks to hell.

The legend of the Caldeira do Santo Cristo

The Azorean island of São Jorge is famous for its picturesque fajãs, small promontories at the foot of the steep cliffs, found mainly on the northern side of the island. Secluded and not easily accessible, they were used as summer pastures and for fishing since the beginning of the island's settlement – if one discards the occasional visits paid by curious pirates.

One fajã offers a particularly charming attraction in the form of a crater-shaped lagoon right next to the mighty surf of the ocean waves. In its calm waters, cockles thrive and are harvested to accompany favorite local dishes. Outside the calm waters of the lagoon, one can collect limpets on the rocky shore or fish for sharptoothed morays in the coastal coves.

On clear days in late spring, two neighboring islands of the central group, Graciosa and Terceira, are easily discernible. Although Terceira appears to be relatively close to São Jorge, the two islands are separated by an immeasurably deep trench on the ocean floor. In the mountains hidden under the deceptive water surface, a giant octopus is said to be lurking and, at irregular intervals, snatches unsuspecting fishing boats that disappear in this Azorean island triangle never to be seen again. One could even assume that a dynasty of these fearsome sea monsters is residing in the rugged underwater landscape, because accounts of giant octopus attacks frightening the wits of the hardiest sailors have been reported since the first navigators scoured the Azorean seas.

Completely unfamiliar with these lurking dangers, one beautiful summer day, a fisherman was absolutely enthralled by the sight of the peaceful lagoon at the foot of the steep cliff, which took him hours to descend. Finally, he caught his breath at the shore of the calm waters of the lagoon, separated from the rolling swell of the heaving ocean. Just when he was about to comfortably settle down to choose his bait, his roaming gaze came to rest on a statue of Christ, halfway submerged in the clear water of the lagoon.

Excitedly, the fisherman totally forgot why he had come down here in the first place. He reverently lifted the statue out of the water and hurried home as fast as the steep path would allow him to move. The whole family was overjoyed about the treasured flotsam and arranged a beautifully decorated corner in their best room for the Santo Cristo to rest and be venerated.

To everybody's consternation, however, the very next morning, it had vanished. Eventually, they found it at the shore of the fajã's lagoon, and they carefully carried it back to its cosy place of honor.

However, twice more the statue disappeared, only to return to the enticing lagoon.

Finally, the people relented to the statue's stubbornness and decided to build a chapel close to the sheltering cliff. When they tried to carry the stones for the building in that direction, these became so heavy that the men could not lift them anymore. Yet again, the islanders reconsidered and ended up erecting the chapel for the Santo Cristo close to the place where the statue had been found.

In the meantime, the fajã was always referred to as the Caldeira do Santo Cristo, and that is the name by which it is still known today. The strong will of the statue needs to be matched by the curious visitor, because the walking trail to the Fajã do Santo Cristo requires physical fitness even as it rewards the hardy with breathtaking panoramic views.

One cold winter night, when dark clouds were chasing across the sky and the wind was ripping at the steep cliff, a priest feared for the safety of the statue and tried to take it to the safety of his own home, but as much as he tried, pulled and pushed, the statue could not be moved. As if glued to its place, it would not budge. The mighty storm passed by without harming the chapel, and when the following morning, the sexton checked to see if the Santo Cristo had survived unharmed, he had no difficulty at all in lifting it for inspection. What did I say about eternal secrets remaining to be uncovered in the isolated island archipelago of the Azores?

Today, there is no doubt in anybody´s mind that the Santo Cristo's choice to become the protector of this fajã turned out to be a divine blessing.

Urzelina, Lina´s heather

Once upon a time, on top of the mountain range that looks like São Jorge's backbone and gives the Azorean island the aspect of a primeval lizard resting in the ocean, Prince Romualdo held court in a majestic castle. The wild orgies and lavish banquets that took place there were causing cacophony ample enough to be heard by the suffering population working hard at its foot to support such lavish lifestyle.

One morning, the regal trumpet was blown to start yet another extravagant hunting party. Down came the frolicking courtiers with loud bravado, accompanied by innumerable servants lugging opulent accessories. With sweat trickling from their foreheads, the people working in the fields watched them disappear in the treacherous heath. But suddenly, wild pigeons flew up in fright, as the colorful scarves of the prince's lover were torn by the untamed bush, and she went missing. Immediately, the hunt was called off. Yet, no amount of searching could find her. In the silent night, the once boisterous frolickers solemnly wove their way back to the castle. The prince locked himself in his quarters. Only his breaking voice was heard sobbing: "Lina! Oh, Lina!"

For days, the inconsolable prince scoured the rugged countryside, until one evening, when dusk was starting to engulf the Azorean islands, he stumbled on a gruesome sight: at the bottom of a steep ravine, his beloved Lina lay, smashed by the weight of her favorite white horse, a pained grimace distorting her fine features. Anguish pounding in his heart, the prince descended into the treacherous depths. In desperation, he kissed his dead lover and cut off one of her shining blond curls, carefully plaiting it together with a sprig of blooming heather.

His heart and soul were broken. He had all doors and windows bolted in the castle. No joyous word was to be heard in his surroundings. The courtiers started to call the plant in the plait that the prince always held close to him Urze de Lina, Lina's heather.

It did not take long for the prince to succumb to his devastating loss and resulting sadness. After his death, the court returned to its lustful excesses, tyrannizing the working population more than ever. But then God sent a mighty punishment. A volcano erupted right under the castle's premises, and its lava flowed all the way down to the ocean. Only one settlement amidst heather growing wild was left untouched. Its inhabitants, remembering the tragic fate of the haughty prince, renamed it Urze de Lina. Nowadays, after much use and wear, that name has been contracted to Urzelina. Each generation, girls are born here bearing the name Lina. And they grow and blossom, and wait for their prince who will love them eternally.

Every day the sea demands one sacrifice

Right from the beginning of the first settlements in the Azores, limpets, at that time abundant sea food in all of the islands, became very popular and a much appreciated delicacy, offering a welcome departure from the daily culinary routine. The islanders, scouring the coastline at low tide, enjoyed the relaxing time collecting the much sought-after treat as they jumped from boulder to boulder with the waves nipping at their toes.

One day, a man from Rosais on the island of São Jorge that, together with Terceira, Pico, Faial and Graciosa, constitutes the central group of the Azorean archipelago, decided to surprise his family by collecting limpets for the evening meal. Carefully, he hopped from one algae-covered stone to the next slippery wet stone. The low tide had left behind some shallow ponds, in which he also found water snails that he eagerly added to the limpets in his wicker basket. Attentively, the man never averted his gaze scanning the breathing ocean, but suddenly the gurgling waves seemed to whisper: "The sea comes, and the sea goes. And where is the human being that does not come?"

At first, the man thought he had not heard right, but when he bent down to pluck some more limpets from a water-washed rock, the spray murmured again: "The sea comes, and the sea goes. And where is the human being that does not come?"

The man started shivering in the cooling ocean breeze. He looked around suspiciously and realized that the tide was coming in. As his basket was as good as filled, he just dared to hop to one more lava rock where he spotted the biggest and juiciest limpets he had come across all day. The water was lapping at his feet, and he knew it was time to leave. When he had already reached the dry beach, the waves were again swishing at his back: "The sea comes, and the sea goes. And where is the human being that does not come?"

He reached the coastal path out of breath, the heavily loaded basket in his hand. A neighbor was just about to descend, still eager to collect some limpets for supper. The friends agreed that as the tide was coming in, the neighbor should not waste any time.

Thus, the neighbor nimbly rushed down to the waterfront, where the best limpet rocks were already threatened to be covered by the cooling ocean. The wicker basket was jerked high, as the neighbor balanced from one wet stone to the next. His left foot slid off a slippery boulder; the sea danced around his left knee. Quickly, he bent down to take off some particularly juicy limpets already submerged by the cleansing spray of the vast ocean.

The neighbor never saw the wave that swept him off his feet. The undertow pulled him out into the open sea and the strong current never granted him a fighting chance. Quietly, his wicker basket floated to the bottom of the ocean.

After the man's family had finished their sumptuous evening meal, they sat outside watching the spectacular performance of the colorful sunset. They were not expecting the neighbor's wife, who rounded the corner with a concerned frown on her face, looking for her husband. That was when the man remembered the whispering sounds of the swishing waves before he had met the neighbor.

Until midnight, the neighbor's friends went looking for him. However, the old people already knew what had happened: When God created the Earth, the water had asked for a human being or a handful of soil as a daily tribute. United in their grief, the mourning relatives and friends understood that the ocean had just been waiting for the neighbor as the sacrifice chosen that day.

Treacherous flies

Whenever an economical or a political crisis made life unbearable in the Azorean islands, emigration became the only way to survive. Most of the time, men were the first to leave and look for safe havens abroad.

And so it was that two young men from São Jorge, who shared not a cent between them, decided to board a ship and try their luck in America. At the end of their voyage, they decided to go their separate ways, but arranged to meet again before returning home. One of the emigrants diligently worked and saved, never turning down any opportunity to make money. The other one rejoiced in finally earning money to spend, but only worked when necessity forced him to interrupt his leisurely lifestyle.

As previously agreed, the two friends met shortly before embarking to sail home. Time flew by, as they told each other about their adventurous lives in the exciting New World. Only too soon, the poor emigrant realized that he would cast a sad figure in comparison to his well-to-do friend once their reached their island. Unscrupulously, he devised a plan to kill his countryman in order to acquire his riches.

All too late, the deceived friend perceived his greedy companion's murderous intentions. There were no witnesses, the victim's eyes were closing, a tear of disbelief and hurt not rousing any feelings. And with his dying breath, the slain friend prophesied that the flies, already settling on him, would give the murderer away, redeem the heartless betrayal.

In cold blood, the villain returned to São Jorge and boasted with the riches that had been accumulated by his slain friend. He had a sprawling house built on the south shore of the island and, finally, had the means to ask for the hand of a young woman who had refused him before. In the afternoons, they would sit behind their house, talking and sharing home-grown wine with friends and neighbors, while looking over to the island of Pico and its spectacular mountain.

One late afternoon, when their guests had already left to be on time for dinner, the untrustworthy friend started giggling while leisurely hitting at the flies dancing around him in circles. His wife had just been watching the sun set, hoping to glimpse the rare green glimmer, said to be seen when the sun vanished in the watery horizon, as it is cherished as an omen of good luck in the Azores. However, as it had eluded her, her husband tried to console her, contentedly reminiscing that he had already benefitted from enough fortunate incidents in his lifetime. In a jovial mood, he leaned forward and confided the secret of his riches to her.

Of course, it did not take his wife long before she had to discuss these scandalous revelations with her best friend, who happened to be married to the highest-ranking law-enforcement officer on the island. In no time, the news of the outrageous deceit spread all over São Jorge, and the police friend was forced to arrest the clandestine murderer. Thus, the dead man's prophesy of flies betraying the gruesome deed came true, and the heinous crime was dutifully punished.

Envy is a lamentable human trait that can also be found in the isolation of the charming Azorean archipelago. However, in this small world, words spread fast; secrets are hard to keep. And yet, the gruesome atrocities caused by marauding pirates were shouted out into the wide world. Harmonious understandings between looting pirates and the bartering island population were not always publicized with equal fervor. Everybody knows, but nobody tells.

Pico

The whaler

It was a beautiful sunny day in June. All over the Azorean island of Pico the men were leisurely reaping their corn and harvesting their potatoes. The women wasted no time in transforming these succulent fruits of their generous soil into mouth-watering fish-and-potato dishes and delicious maize puddings and bread.

Suddenly, the languid bucolic scene changed to a hectic pace of excitement. The signal of the whale lookout was heard far and wide, and the men dropped their hoes and spades, tied the donkeys carrying heavy burdens at the stone walls separating the fields and hurried to the harbor. Hardly did the women have time to slip the food parcels into their hands. Women and children watched with happy anticipation as the whaling boats disappeared on the horizon.

With awe, the whalers approached their peacefully drifting prey. It was a sperm whale of extraordinary size. Not only would it render more than 100 barrels of oil, but it also posed a challenge that made every whaler strain his muscles. Expertly the harpooner in the front boat poised himself for the deadly assault. He hit his target perfectly and caught it by surprise.

The injured whale went wild with pain and frantically dived to escape its fate. The first reel of rope disappeared into the depths of the ocean, the spare one following at a maddening pace. Before his friends could stop him, the proud harpooner, a giant of a man, tied the end of the rope around his waist, just before he was pulled overboard.

Until darkness fell, the boats spread out and searched to find the whaler's body, but whale and man had vanished. The moon was already glittering on the nervous waves when the whaling boats returned to the harbor. Joy and excitement gave way to disbelief and profound sadness. The harpooner's family went into mourning, and neighbors and friends joined them to weep and moan about the tragic death. In respectfully hushed voices, the other whalers retold their friend's audacious feat.

The next morning, some boats left to appease public conscience and as a last attempt to grant the formidable harpooner an honorable funeral. Suddenly, the surprised men spotted a dark speck on the horizon. Hastily, they steered in its direction and could hardly believe what they found.

On top of the gigantic corpse of the sperm whale, the long-lost whaler was leaning against his harpoon that was solidly fastened in the whale's blubber. Leisurely, he was smoking one of his favorite cigars, but at the sight of his approaching friends, he indignantly folded his arms over his chest and greeted them gruffly: "Only now do you arrive? After leaving me waiting all night long!" Every American reader, of course, knows that this whaler was a close relative of the formidable Davy Crockett.

The fisherman and the *labregos*

Until the beginning of the 20th century, the population of Pico firmly believed in the existence of *labregos*, ill-meaning gnomes, who sported the habit of leaving the ocean on February 2, the night of Nossa Senhora das Candeias, to hide in the wooded interior of this Azorean island not to return to the sea until eight months later. In these nights of lingering danger, the islanders would not venture out of their homes, if at all possible, but would lock and bolt their doors for safety and avoid going to sea, or even close to the shore.

However, one man from Calheta decided to go fishing that very night in February. Either he really experienced the dire necessity to catch fish for sustenance, or he simply belonged to that group of people who always needs to boast that they are not scared of anything. In any case, the weather proved to be reasonably calm, although it was one of these pitch-black nights in which the moon and the stars seem to choose the night-time saving mode.

As soon as the fisherman had sorted out his tackle and had comfortably lit his hand-rolled cigar, he extinguished his torch and leisurely swung his leg over his fishing rod. Contently relishing his tobacco, the fisherman patiently waited for fish to bite. Instead, he suddenly heard hoarse voices whispering behind his back: "What are you waiting for? Just throw him into the sea!" Instantly, another voice, dripping with disappointment, replied: "I wish I could, but I can't. He ate garlic, oak-apple and cinder-cake."

The fisherman became frightened out of his wits. His hair stood on end, his cigar dropped out of his open mouth and sizzled among the wet pebbles under his feet. It took him hardly any time to grab his fishing gear and sprint home as fast as his feet would carry him. At home, he bolted all doors and windows. He still strained his ears when he was safely tucked away in bed, but, of course, the *labregos* did not disturb the security of his house.

The next morning, everybody was already talking about the fisherman's haunting experience, because all Azorean islands are small enough for word to spread faster than it would ever be possible via modern technology. Everybody's private life soon becomes public knowledge. After this fateful night, the older generation took the opportunity to point out that the old traditions and sayings should better be respected and not haughtily discarded and treated with disdain. Nowadays, children attentively act on their elders' advice and diligently stay at home on those nights of mischief and danger. Besides, out at sea or on the beach there would be no electricity to allow them to play their internet and PlayStation games, or would there?

Nesquim's Bay

Long ago, many merchant ships passing through the Azores transported valuable goods and fabulous treasures from the New World to Europe through the waters surrounding the Azorean islands. Atlantic traveling is unpredictable at the best of times, and because of the notorious winter storms, most voyages were made between the months of May and October. However, the violent storms in September enjoyed an especially frightful reputation.

One dark night in early fall, nature's fury decided to unleash itself over the central group of the Azorean archipelago, and caught a ship laden with valuable timber totally by surprise, as it was just passing the southern coast of Pico. For a while, the vessel floundered in utter distress between the heaving waves. Then the stowage lost its equilibrium, causing the ship to lean to one side, inviting the greedy sea to fill it in no time. Most of the crew drowned when the vessel sank to the bottom of the ocean on this ill-fated night.

Disoriented in the pitch-black turmoil of the raging storm, three sailors helplessly followed the lead of the ship's dog, called Nesquim, that instinctively sensed the proximity of the shoreline. Soon, the exhausted men heard the surf crashing against the pebble beach. They saw the vague contours of a towering cliff looming above their bobbing heads. In a last effort, they dragged themselves onto the stony beach where the light-coated Nesquim was shaking the water out of his dripping hair. After a prayer of heartfelt gratitude, the three sailors instantly called this small promontory after the loyal dog that had saved their lives, Nesquim's Bay.

The three men eventually moved to different parts of the island, but a small settlement developed where Nesquim had led them ashore. The dog continued to live among its intrepid fishermen and whalers who became known all over the island for their ingenuity and resilience. The dog's intelligence and courage were still re-membered long after his death in the small bay of Calheta do Nesquim.

Senhor Jesus and Senhora Santa Barbara

After one of those infamous wild storms at the onset of the winter season, a fisherman found a wooden box washed ashore, close to the harbor of Ribeiras on the Azorean island of Pico. They pulled the box out of the reach of the returning tide and tried to open it. However, the box resisted every attempt to reveal its contents.

Full of curiosity, the children were playing around it, poking here and there, shy and yet daring at the same time. Everybody watched in amazement as one little boy, innocently probing around to open the lid, suddenly held it in his hands without having exerted the slightest effort. The onlookers were even more surprised when they perceived a statue of the crucified Jesus inside. Full of awe, they immediately christened the miraculous find Senhor Jesus, Lord Jesus.

Before dusk fell, some women collecting limpets among the rocks that the tide had left high and dry on the pebble beach detected a statue of Santa Barbara. The inhabitants of the settlement were elated about the two religious items of flotsam reaching their island on the same day. As they had two churches, they decided to place Senhora Santa Barbara in the church close to the harbor of Ribeiras, while the other church was happy to provide a place of honor to Senhor Jesus.

However, the next morning, when the first faithful gathered for morning prayer, they discovered to their great astonishment that the two statues had traded places, although nobody came forward to admit carrying them back and forth. The local priests shook their heads, puzzled, but determined, and had the statues exchanged again. Yet, all determination was to no avail, because for two more nights the statues insisted on going back to the churches they wanted to stay at.

An old spinster, who had difficulties sleeping at night when the full moon was turning the sea into livid silver and the mermaids and werewolves were said to be lurking around full of mischief, even claimed to have watched the two statues cross paths on their nightly trips back to where they had chosen to rest.

At last, the congregations admitted defeat and allowed Senhor Jesus and Senhora Santa Barbara to have their way and determine their own religious settings. Each year, joyous festivities celebrate the miraculous appearance of the two statues. The place where

Senhor Jesus had been washed ashore became known as Santa Cruz. The stone on which the crucified Jesus had been found was considered holy. When, in 1980, the coastline was consolidated with concrete, the stone was removed and, nowadays, you can find it in the middle of the little garden next to the church of Santa Cruz in Pico.

A year of famine

It was a bad year, a year of ravishing hunger caused by a dry spell that had devastated harvests on all the Azorean islands of the central group. The corn never grew, nor matured, and thus there were no seeds to be sown the following year. Calla flowers and fern were used to make bread and puddings. But in the midst of this dire situation of extreme starvation, the inhabitants of Pico never lost their faith in the Holy Spirit. Therefore, the rations set aside for the Holy-Spirit-festivities were never depleted.

Two sisters in Santa Barbara had reserved two sacks of wheat for the communal banquet, and they had stored them high up on a wooden grate so that the rats could not reach them. When, in the end, they had absolutely nothing left to eat, they took a needle and pricked a tiny hole in each sack, thus allowing single grains to be taken out to alleviate the gnawing hunger pangs. By the time the

Holy-Spirit-festivities grew closer, they had not yet taken out more than the amount that was still left in the sacks, but the sacks were definitely no longer full.

One night, they woke up hearing a suspicious noise in their pantry. Quickly, they jumped out of bed, ready to defend their wheat sacks from a potential rat attack. Hardly could they believe their eyes when they saw that both sacks had been filled to the rim. Furthermore, so much had overflowed that several little heaps were piling up on the floor, enough to satisfy their hunger for at least a month or two.

The miraculous incident was generally seen as a blessing granted by the Holy Spirit, impressed by the sisters' selflessness and respect. In fact, even nowadays, local Holy-Spirit-societies still look after the welfare of their communities, never boasting of their life-saving functions, but offering a safe haven to whoever might need one.

The girl who longed to become a witch

One cold winter night on the Azorean island of Pico, some neighbors had gathered around a warming fireplace to spend the evening in pleasant company warding off the chill that was hovering around the little houses of Calheta. Bright-eyed, Aunt Leal was indulging in the educational tales of her youth, while the young girls were much more fascinated by the hair-raising stories of vampires and witches. One 18-year-old girl eventually sighed longingly: "Oh, if only I could be a witch!"

Shortly before midnight, not even the most outrageous accounts of werewolves and saintly miracles managed to suppress the increased yawning in this intimate circle of friends and neighbors. One after the other, they left and went home.

The 18-year-old girl only needed to walk down one short path to reach her parents' home, but she had to pass through a dark alley, and at its entrance, a respectable looking woman joined her and inquired in a hushed voice if she was serious about wanting to become a witch. In the obscurity of the nightly shadows, the girl tried to recognize the woman's face and, quite flustered, stuttered that she had uttered that wish.

All of a sudden, she found herself three kilometers down the road on top of Pico Ruivo. To her great amazement, witches were arriving from all wind directions. They swayed and danced like in a trance around a haughtily grinning billy-goat, who acted as if he were their protector. Whenever they passed him, the witches giggled and reverently kissed his ass. Everybody was in a joyous, festive mood, excitedly anticipating the initiation ceremony of a new member, that of the 18-year-old girl. To her consternation, she was expected to join in the ritual and also kiss the billy-goat's buttocks. Repulsed, she turned away her face distorted by utter disgust, and exclaimed: "Holy Mary, am I supposed to do something as repugnant as that?"

No sooner had she pronounced the Virgin Mary's name, than the grotesque charade evaporated in a cloud of sparks and smoke, and the girl found herself lying in the middle of prickly brambles without a stitch of clothing covering her body. This is how some men found her the next morning on their way to their fields. They immediately understood what had happened that night. They plucked the girl, who was frozen stiff and scratched all over, out of the brambles and wrapped her in their work jackets. Then they accompanied the embarrassed wannabe witch back to her parents' house – and there was thus yet another story to be told on a cold winter night around a warm fireplace.

Faial

The regal crown of Cedros

At the time of the Castilian reign in the Azores, the attacks of marauding pirates coming from northern Africa occurred so frequently that life became hard to bear in the archipelago. Even Faial, one of the islands of the more protected central group, suffered its fair share of devastating raids, so that its inhabitants diligently tried to find ingenious means and ways to repel these unwelcome visitors.

At one time, the defense initiative in Faial was so successful warding off these unruly sailors that during the tumultuous mayhem, the commander of the pirates lost his richly chiseled silver crown. Once the crew had regained its breath in the safety of their ship, the captain deemed it necessary to regroup and try to retrieve the missing regalia. While they were searching for the valuable jewelry in every nook and cranny, the pirates again had to face the fury of the beleaguered residents. However, the crown just seemed to have vanished, and the pirates finally had to retreat in confused bewilderment. When the ship sailed away, the captain vowed never to set foot on this island ever again – a resolution that the residents of Faial would probably not have been sorry to hear.

In the meantime, one sly woman from the village of Cedros sneakily kept a dangerous secret hidden under her skirts. During her pursuit of the fleeing pirates, she had stumbled over the commanding pirate's crown, as her eye caught the glittering of its precious gemstone in the deceptive sunlight. Since the crown was shaped like a smooth ring, not being serrated or pointed in any way, she had pulled it up her left leg as one would push a wedding band onto one's ring finger.

Even after the ship had disappeared on the horizon, that suspicious woman did not remove her hidden find, as if she suspected the pirates to return yet again. However, after a few days, her leg started to swell and discolor, and she eventually succumbed to seeking help. Her leg was bathed with soap made with cinder, and her skin became all slippery, but the regal insignia had no intention of sliding off the woman's leg.

Finally, they resorted to cutting the metal ring off her leg in a painful process that was accompanied by the loud lamenting of the crafty woman. Afterwards, of course, the crown needed to be soldered with great care. The precious gemstone set in it never lost its lustre, but the blurred smudge of the chiseled design clearly betrays where the silver had to be cut and mended. Every year, the crown enjoys a place of honor during the Holy-Spirit-festivities. However, for the procession an exact copy of it is carried through the village of Cedros. One can never trust these pirates, can one? They might come back to Faial one day in order to reclaim their regal insignia.

Buried alive

About 200 years ago, the daughter of the aristocratic family Quadros of Horta, on the Azorean island of Faial, made the unwise decision to follow her heart and fall in love with a young man who had nothing to his name but his intelligence and hard working ethics. While Amelia was expected to follow the path many aristocratic girls had to take at that time, which inescapably enclosed them behind convent walls, young Alfredo had already managed to secure a respectable position in an English company, which was trading the famous Verdelho wine from the island of Pico.

Although the two young people fell head over heels in love with one another, their feelings never stood a chance in the eyes of Amelia's family of landed gentry. Consequently, the nobleman Quadros forced his daughter to start her novitiate against her will, even though she implored him to spare her that fate.

The nuns of the convent of Sao Joao thus spent their days trying to interest Amelia in religious studies, while at night the stubborn girl kept dreaming of Alfredo's fiery kisses on her burning lips. Shortly before the completion of the novitiate, the honorable nobleman came to check on his daughter in the convent. Yet again, Amelia made it absolutely clear that she had no intention of becoming a nun, ever. She even threatened to refuse taking the binding oath. As a reply, the haughty nobleman cast a menacing glance at his rebellious offspring and retorted sharply that he would bury his daughter up to the hilt of his sabre and leave her in the ground for eight days if she dared tarnish their respectable family name.

In desperation, Amelia wrote to Alfredo, beseeching him to help her. However, Alfredo's instant reply was made on the verge of his departure to England, where he was sent to conduct important business transactions. Deserted by family and friends, the desolate girl slid into deep depression.

On the day of the completion of the novitiate, the convent of Sao Joao was humming with festive anticipation. Only Amelia felt like fainting when she was called to take the binding oath. At her side, her cold-hearted father reminded her of her obligations. Incredulously, Amelia realized that no one understood her suffering. With draining strength, she whispered: "Honorable father, on thy wish,

I will be buried alive." Her golden curls slid to the ground, severed by the relentless scissors cutting her off from worldly life. Her heart and mind broke, when she uttered the lifeless words of the binding oath, and blood trickled over her crimson lips staining her immaculately white handkerchief.

The nun Amelia da Purificação never regained enough strength to write to Alfredo. When in the following spring, the roses she had planted had blossomed into full bloom, the young aristocratic nun died without anybody caring that her heart stopped beating.

At first, Alfredo felt bereaved, but soon after, he married a charming young English woman, the daughter of a wealthy merchant family. The right honorable nobleman Quadros lived to a ripe old age, loved and respected by one and all. One morning, he was found lying motionless in his bed, apparently dead. With great pomp and circumstance, he was laid to rest in the stately tomb of the Quadros family in Carmo.

Some years later, the tomb's leaking entrance hall needed to be repaired. When the masons removed the plates of the ceiling, they found a skeleton crouching on the uppermost step of the staircase. They immediately contacted the verger who checked the church registry and concluded that the gruesome find could be none other than the nobleman Quadros, as he had been the last one to be put to rest in the tomb.

Thus, the man who had his daughter buried alive by condemning her to the confines of a convent, ended his own life being buried alive, too – by sheer coincidence, or divine justice? You can find families with this noble name on various Azorean islands. Yet, none of them seems to be able to trace their lineage back to that noble gentleman described in this well-known legend. Well now!

The oven that was spared from the fire

In Faial, one of the islands in the central group of the Azorean archipelago, there lived a poor woman who was the mother of many children. In order to feed them, she had to bake corn bread and corn cakes every single day, but afterwards there was always enough left to give to those who were even needier than her in the little village of Capelos.

When, in 1672, a volcano erupted in Faial, the population fled in panic, as the molten lava crushed and covered everything in its path. Houses were destroyed, forests burned to the ground and harvests incinerated in the well-kept fields. As unexpectedly as the earth had started to shake and spew up its fiery contents, quietness returned, and the lava cooled and froze as if a spell had been cast.

Tentatively, the displaced population returned to see what had happened to their properties and possessions. Capelos turned out to be completely covered by the glowing equalizer. Only the oven of the poor woman with the numerous children had been spared. Serenely, it stood untouched, surrounded by the petrified lava stream. The ladle to push the bread into the fire was leaning at its side, ready to bake new bread and cake in order to satisfy the hunger of the poor and needy.

The bean pudding of the monks in Horta

Not that long ago, a very rich family lived on the Azorean island of Faial. Their only son grew up pampered and convinced that the world revolved around him. He ended up being so conceited that he even refused the lucrative marriage proposals his father was so diligently arranging for him. Haughtily, the son found fault with each one of the young ladies. When, at last, the father realized that his son had no inclinations to secure an increase of the family fortune and carry on its name, he made his son join the local monastery.

The spoiled young man did not take to the Spartan life of a monk easily, and learned to cherish the arrivals of the food parcels that his parents sent him on special occasions. Often he felt desperate cravings for one of his favorite desserts with which his parents' cook used to pamper him during his childhood.

One day, he received a parcel of dried fruits and a variety of delicious food items. Overwhelmed by sweet memories, the noble monk used the contents of the parcel to imitate what he remembered his parents' cook doing so long ago in his carefree childhood. Tentatively he mixed white beans with eggs, almonds and candied lemon peel and then pushed the dough into the monastery's oven.

To his utter delight, the pudding turned out to be a success, and from then on, the brethren regularly ended their festive meals with this special treat. Soon, word spread and the recipe escaped the confines of the monastery walls to be enjoyed and appreciated by the general population. If you want to know what this dessert tastes like, just order a Pudim de Feiãoj dos Frades do Convento da Horta. Yummy, yummy, indeed!

Which sacristy X?

On the eve of August 14, 1760, the Jesuit monks were busy preparing the festive celebrations of Mary's Ascension. The town of Horta on the Azorean island of Faial was bathed in the golden sunlight just before dusk would set in, softening its contours to create an atmosphere of comfortable peacefulness. While a stately Portuguese warship was dropping anchor in a sheltered bay of the harbor, the Jesuit monks rushed around to put on display the splendid decorations of the monastery for this festive day. Innumerable candles twinkled through stained-glass lamp shades, the valuable ceremonial utensils glittered and gleamed throwing light reflections on the walls and ceiling, the golden tassels sparkling for attention.

And yet, the brethren moved at an unaccustomed pace, their gestures hectic, their voices subdued. Even the liturgical ceremonies seemed abbreviated, for they were well-aware of the danger that was lurking on the powerful Portuguese ship, swaying so calmly in the darkening harbor.

Attentively, the ship's captain was watching the festive bustle as the inhabitants of Horta streamed into the church to hear mass. Not one was missing, the rich and the poor alike gathered in the Jesuit monastery to listen to God's word. Everyone knew that the enlightened teaching of the Jesuits with their political aspirations had provoked the unforgiving hatred of the mighty Marques de Pombal.

The Jesuits had a dreadful foreboding. They thought it better to prepare for the worst. After the general public had dispersed, they returned to the darkening church, accompanied only by an African servant, each one of them clutching a hoe or a spade. In the flickering light of the remaining candles, they dug a deep trench. In it, they deposited the valuable church decorations that just a short while ago had made God's temple shine in utmost splendor. Thus, they buried the delicate monstrance sprinkled with sparkling gemstones, as well as the candelabras made of solid silver, a magnificent cup adorned with nine precious gemstones representing the nine Azorean islands and the irreplaceable sacrament light. Then there were boxes, full of gold coins and other valuable assets pertaining to the Jesuit monastery. All of them were laid into the sweetly smelling soil and covered with stone slabs to safeguard this treasure from the greedy hands of the envious adversaries.

After having accomplished this precautionary deed, the monks withdrew to spend a restless night tossing around in their cots, seeking God's guidance. None of them knew what the future would hold in store for them when the new morning sun rose to another summer day of serene tranquillity. Tension hovered in the air when the monks went to hear the first mass on the holy day of Mary's Ascension. As soon as the liturgy ended, church and monastery were surrounded by the Portuguese troops. The Jesuits had no means to stand up to this act of intimidation. They humbly left the sacristy, united as a group. They were made to board the warship, carrying nothing but their breviaries in their folded hands. Anchors were weighed, and an accommodating breeze blew into the proudly billowing sails. Elegantly, the ship slid out of the harbor of Horta.

The population of Faial was never informed about the destiny of the Jesuit monks, but they learned about it anyway. On his deathbed, the loyal African servant confided to a nun of the Gloria Convent the whereabouts of the legendary Jesuit treasure. She never told anyone, but after she passed away, a time-worn piece of paper was found among her scanty possessions. It held these enigmatic words: *The African told me that he helped to bury the boxes with the treasure of the Jesuit monastery in the sacristy X.* As tantalizing as this weathered scrap of information was, it told little about which one of the five sacristies the African was talking about.

Flores

Our Lady of the Pirates or Our Lady of Ships

The year 1672 was a year like many others at a time when the Azores were hardly ever allowed any reprieve. If it was not the fierce Atlantic storms that battered them, then pirates' actions resulted in fright and fear among the sparse island populations. These wild sailors looted and robbed, destroyed and killed, taking food rations as well as valuable treasures from private homes and churches alike.

As peaceful as one morning in early January seemed to dawn, just as alarmed the inhabitants of Flores became when they spotted a large fleet of ships on the horizon heading straight to their little community of Santa Cruz. In all, they counted 27 ships hoisting the Dutch flag, and when the crews disembarked with their weapons into their small boats, the islanders instantly perceived that they did not stand a fleeting chance. They would obviously be outnumbered by men and arms, and their fate seemed to be sealed.

Resignation set in, and they gathered for a final prayer in their church, the Igreja da Conceição. And there, the priest appealed to their fighting spirit. He encouraged them to face death while at the same time remaining steadfast in their belief. Obediently, the congregation hoisted the statue of Mary onto their shoulders and moved in procession towards the harbor where the invaders were about to land.

The Dutch had nearly reached the shallow shoreline, and with dread, the parishioners watched the advancing sailors swing their formidable weapons, shouting in disdain and hurling insults by way of threatening greetings. Hovering over the heads of the shaken procession, the statue of Mary was smiling down mildly at the wild scene.

All of a sudden, like a bolt out of the blue, a ravaging storm caught everybody by utter surprise. The rain drenched the dumbfounded islanders, the wind blew so strong from an adverse direction that no amount of rowing helped the attackers to succeed in reaching the shore that had once looked so close. Instead, their little boats were pushed out to sea, the mounting waves tossing them up and down like nutshells. Hastily they scrambled to return to the safety of their ships, and they could not wait to weigh their anchors and move out to sea before the wind would smash them against the sharp rocks of the coastline.

With a gracious smile on her lips, the statue of Mary watched the pirates retreat. The little island congregation was wind-swept, but filled with eternal gratitude. For centuries, each January, a procession was re-enacted as a reminder of how Our Lady of Ships, as the congregation renamed their statue of Mary, saved the inhabitants of Santa Cruz in Flores.

Nowadays, the statue can be found in the Igreja da Conceição. It has grown old and venerable, but it has not lost its benevolent smile.

How the village "Caveira", Skull, got its name

In the 16th century, the Azorean island of Flores was passed by many caravels coming from America and Asia, all laden with luxury items destined for the rich markets of continental Europe. The weather and the ocean often played rough, and many a ship capsized when nature's whim unleashed its fierce elements, burying its treasures at the bottom of the sea at places nobody will ever know about. Other times, these caravels were equally unlucky when ruthless pirates attacked and looted them, neither sparing men nor merchandise. Flotsam and jetsam were washed ashore, as were some lucky survivors of such attacks.

One might be forgiven for speculating that the inhabitants of these conveniently situated islands could sometimes not refrain from taking the initiative to intercept some of these precious cargos in order to brighten their harsh lives in the middle of the Atlantic Ocean. In any case, no useful item reaching the shores of these isolated islands was ever rejected, and shipwrecked unfortunates were mostly given shelter and even offered the social support to start new lives among friends.

This is what happened to a sailor called Demetrius, who found himself washed ashore on Flores one stormy night in February. He was frozen stiff and starving, but the inhabitants took good care of him, and soon he fully recovered and turned into a valuable asset to the local community. It did not take long for Demetrius to marry and raise a bunch of healthy kids.

However, although he became totally integrated in the social life surrounding him, Demetrius never converted to Catholicism. He stubbornly denied the existence of purgatory and maintained that the soul lived within the human blood. He believed that at the moment of death, the soul would leave the human body and move into a bird which he understood to be the personification of the goddess of death, called Morana. By virtue of a sweet melody, the bird would ease the soul's transfer into the eternal dream.

Demetrius never bothered anybody with his believes, enjoyed good health until old age, then suddenly fell ill and died. At the moment of his death, a wagtail was seen to fly to the nearest myrica faya, the most common tree in the Azores at that time, but the bird remained silent. Demetrius' wife became preoccupied because the bird had not sung. But once her husband was buried on top of the nearest hill, the episode was quickly forgotten.

However, soon after, neighbors and friends were shocked to see a skull, gleaming ominously from inside, on that very hilltop where Demetrius had been laid to rest. The inhabitants of the little community immediately interpreted this apparition as a plea for help to admit Demetrius' soul into purgatory. During mass, they said prayers for his soul and came together to pray the rosary.

To their delight, they did not have to wait long for the wagtail to fly to the myrica faya, where it sang a most melodious tune. At the same time, the gleaming image of the skull vanished from the hilltop, and with a sigh of relief Demetrius' family and friends assumed that his soul had finally found peace. A commemorative slab of stone with the image of a skull was placed where the eerie apparition had been seen. This episode proved to be of such importance to this community that henceforward it became known as Caveira, Skull.

How the "Cana da India" found its way to Flores

About 200 years ago, an upright and honest fisherman lived with his wife and only daughter, both called Maria, on the northwestern Azorean island of Flores. They made do with whatever the sea provided for their sustenance and were happy and satisfied with their lives. One dark Friday night, this domestic bliss was suddenly destroyed without them even noticing it.

One of their closest neighbors happened to be a witch, and that fateful night she felt death knocking at the door. The two Marias considered it their neighborly duty to keep the old woman company at this time of final agony. On her deathbed, the old witch became distressed because there was no kin on whom to bequeath her magical powers. In utter desperation, she clutched her magic pouch and screeched: "Who will catch what I have to hand down?" She tossed the pouch into the air and, with that, she drew her last breath. The fisherman's wife was gripped with pity for the old woman in her final agony and caught the pouch without knowing what she was doing, for as soon as the pouch changed hands, the two Marias turned into witches.

At first, nobody noticed anything suspicious. Then, one morning, the fisherman found his boat dripping wet, although he had not been out fishing that night. The following night he went to bed as usual, but only pretended to sleep. To his amazement, at midnight, his wife and daughter left their beds and went outside. Stealthily, the fisherman slunk out of his bed and followed them. No sooner had he hid under the bundle of fishing nets in his boat, when mother and daughter jumped in, too. In a rough voice they commanded: "Off you go with your passengers!" Promptly, the boat slid into the water and off they sped at lightning speed.

In hardly any time, they reached a beach in India, and before the fisherman could fully recover from his surprise, the two Marias had disappeared into the fields full of Cana da India. Carefully, he hastened behind them, always watching out that he would not be detected. He found his wife and daughter sitting together with two strangers, eating and drinking to their hearts' content. When they started to swirl around to wild dancing tunes, he held his breath and could hardly contain himself.

Although he was beside himself with rage and worry, he realized quite well that if somebody was to believe his story, he needed proof. Silently, he crept back to the beach, broke off a piece of Cana da India and hid in the boat again. He did not have to wait long for the two Marias to return. Again, they commanded in an authoritative voice:" Off you go with your passengers!" And the boat sped through the water at such a velocity that the fisherman feared losing his senses.

Before dawn broke, the fishing boat, still dripping wet from its midnight excursion, rested at its usual place, and mother and daughter slept in their beds, the very picture of female innocence. Yet, the fisherman knew better and went straight to the priest. He told him the whole story and showed him the piece of Cana da India. The priest did believe this incredulous account and accompanied the fisherman to his humble cottage. Before the two Marias awakened and stirred, the priest had already said blessings over them and over the fishing boat. The fisherman saw smoke coming out of the magic pouch as it disintegrated into ashes. To his relief, the fisherman realized that the evil spell had been lifted from his wife and daughter.

The piece of Cana da India could not be stopped, though. It easily adapted to the Azorean climate and freely spread all over the Azorean islands. The favorable weather conditions and the fertile volcanic soil have helped many flotsam from far-away places to settle in their hospitable new environment. Or did you already know that the decorative floral representative of the Azores, the hydrangea, is by no means an endemic plant of the archipelago?

The mermaid of Ponta Ruiva

One afternoon in the 16th century, on the northern coast of the Azorean island of Flores, a young fisherman went to the shore to fish, as was his custom. It did not take long for the sound of the lapping waves to make him feel drowsy. He was about to fall asleep, when all of a sudden, he heard a sweet voice singing a heartbreaking song in a language he could not understand. He searched behind all the boulders around him, but then he decided to return home as the sun had already set and the thin sliver of the moon did not provide enough light to help him in his search.

Over and over, the young fisherman told his story of the enchanting melody, and soon he was convinced that it could only have been the alluring song of a mermaid. His friends laughed at him and teased him by saying that the mermaid had already cast her spell over him, as he was talking on and on about that mysterious evening. Angrily, the young fisherman decided to prove to them that he had, indeed, heard a mermaid.

The following afternoon, he took his fishing gear and set off to the spot where he had been surprised by the enchanting voice. No sooner had he cast his line, when the mysterious voice started to sing again. This time the young fisherman did not waste any time.

He abandoned his fishing rod and steadfastly moved in the direction from where the melancholic song came.

He was certainly surprised to find, not a mermaid, but a beautiful young ginger-haired woman with no fishtail sitting on a boulder by the sea, looking at the sun that was already vanishing in the ocean. The woman's hair seemed to be ablaze as it had the color of leaping flames, while her blue eyes seemed to reflect the ocean depths. Never had the young fisherman seen a human being with such fair, nearly transparent skin, with freckles dancing all over to a mischievous tune.

When the young woman saw the fisherman, her voice stopped and she sat still, petrified with fear. Patiently, the young man made her understand that he meant no harm. In the end, she believed him and explained that she was, indeed, no mermaid, but an Irish woman. A pirate ship had held her captive, and one night, as they were passing the island at close proximity, she had managed to quietly jump overboard as soon as the moon had begun hiding behind the clouds.

Proudly, the young fisherman led the Irish girl back to his parents' house. None of his family or friends had ever seen a woman as beautiful as this girl. Nobody was laughing about the young fisherman anymore, and it did not take long for him to move into his own house with the Irish beauty as his wife.

Many kids were born to this happy couple, and they all looked like their mother, ginger-haired, blue-eyed and with such a fair complexion that the freckles seemed to dance to a merry tune on the translucent white skin. Because of this family, the tip of land where they lived and still live became known as Ponta Ruiva, tip of the ginger-haired. Today, if you take some time to sit there by the shore, admiring the glorious sunset, surrounded by the orange and blue of the bedazzling sky, a fisherman might pass you on his way to the water's edge. You will be surprised to see that his hair is the color of leaping flames, his eyes the color of the deep-blue sea and his skin so white that the freckles on it are dancing to a mischievous tune.

The tragedy at the Abyss of the seven Marias, the Baixa das Sete Marias

Right from the beginning of the first settlements in the Azores, limpets were regarded as a delicious supplement to the inhabitants' daily diet. On the northwestern Azorean island of Flores, young women loved to meet, after they had finished their chores, in order to go to the shore, where they gaudily jumped from boulder to boulder while collecting the tasty shellfish.

One day, a group of seven girls from the village of Lajes also decided to pursue this pleasant pastime close to a place called Mosteiros. Talking and joking, they set out to frolic around until dusk would call them home. Not surprisingly, all seven girls were called Maria, a name that has proved to be a favorite in the Azores all through the centuries.

Traditionally, names get inherited, so that Maria José (Maria Joseph) or Maria João (Maria John) already had aunts or great aunts bestowed with the same name. Maybe it should be pointed out that Maria do Céu (Maria of Heaven) and Maria da Conceição (Maria of Conception) most of the time do not have parents who will force them to join a convent. And before you get your expectations up, I also want to admit that Maria do Mar (Maria of the Sea) is by no means the daughter of a genuine mermaid – not even in our legends.

Back to Flores, the seven Marias reached the sea at low tide and happily clambered all the way down to the very edge of the licking waves. Being the best of friends, they had great fun and laughed and shrieked when the red and green algae tickled their bare feet.

However, these algae were wet and quite slippery, and so it was not too long before one of the Marias slipped, and slid into the treacherous waves. Frightened, she tried to find her footing, but the current prevented her from returning to the shore, and forcefully pulled her out to sea. Another Maria, the unfortunate Maria's best friend, observed the screaming woman's plight and jumped into the water to save her. Yet again, the ocean had other plans, and thus she followed the first Maria's fate. The other five Marias, watching their friends being helplessly carried out to sea, grew desperate and did not know where to turn for help. One after the other, they dove into the lurking depths of the ocean, trying to save their friends. One after the other, they were carried away by the mighty tidal current, never to be seen again.

The families and friends of the seven Marias cried their eyes out over this tragedy. For decades to come, everybody shunned the Abyss of the Seven Marias, where the seven friends had lost their lives to the unpredictable Atlantic Ocean. Today, the daring collectors of limpets at this sinister place still make sure that they always keep watchful eyes on the rolling waves and never lose their footing, while the cool sea breeze rushes over their backs reminding them of the tragic fate the seven Marias suffered.

While eating the local delicacy in one of the scenic Azorean restaurant over pleasant conversations with friends, one might easily be unaware of the perturbing fact that these harmless looking crustaceans are responsible for numerous deaths among their collectors every single year even in our day. The sea comes, and the sea goes.

The legend of the dry pond or "Caldeira Seca"

Once upon a time, a very rich family lived on Flores, one of the two northwestern islands of the Azorean archipelago. This family had two sons who were the best of friends. When these sons had become adults, their old father died and bequeathed to them his entire property. Everybody expected the two young men to honor their father's will and cherish his memory in harmony.

Instead, the two sons decided to divide the estate, and as some sections were of greater value than others, they soon began to haggle and argue. Each brother feared being cheated by the other one, each brother yearned to secure the best sections for himself. Distrust replaced friendship, general suspicion culminated in hatred.

One desolate winter morning, they agreed to meet in a distant valley in the interior highlands of the island. Neither brother confided in the other one the true reason for this encounter. And yet, both brothers had made up their minds to pursue the same evil plan: each of them aspired to kill the other.

Each brother resorted to taking a different path to reach their destination. Their progress was unexpectedly fast, as they were both driven by maddening greed and hatred. Both brothers reached the edge of the valley on opposing sides at the same time, and, blind with rage, both of them nearly tumbled into the pond that stretched out in front of them. Both young men blinked with surprise as they found themselves separated by the smooth and calm waters of a pleasant pond that had not been there before. They could not reach each other, nor could they proceed with their plans. Had they forgotten to honor their father's legacy? Was the pond a sign from God to deter the brothers from taking each other's life? Embarrassment rose in both brothers. They lowered their eyes and turned around in shame. With hanging heads, they quietly rode home. There, they promised each other never to let anything break up their friendship, to banish greed and to work together in harmony.

Every winter, the dry valley of Caldeira Seca fills with water, and the clear pond reminds the islanders of the brothers' promise to help each other the best they can.

The seven ponds of Flores

Once upon a time, on the island of Flores, which can be found in the northwestern extremity of the Azorean archipelago, there lived a man whose son was called João. The boy was a good-natured day-dreamer, simple and kind-hearted, just like most people are said to be in Flores.

One day the boy was sent out to fetch a few pails of water from a well quite a distance away. On his way home, he was not paying attention to where he was going. He was, instead, following his own peculiar train of thoughts. All of a sudden, he stood still and started talking to himself: "They say there are beautiful lakes and ponds on other islands. And here, we do not have any. Something needs to be done about it." No sooner said than done. He bent over, emptied one pail into a puddle by the wayside, and lo and behold, a beautiful pond stretched out at his feet.

The boy looked at what he had done with satisfaction. He liked what he saw and decided to turn every puddle he would come across into a charming pond. Of course, he had to go back to the well several times to refill his pails, but he did not mind the effort and dreamily continued his project until, finally, he reached home with two jugs of crystal-clear water.

To this day, the seven ponds of Flores impress their onlooker with their simple beauty. Their water is as clear and sweet as the soul of the little boy who made them.

Corvo

The pirate and fakir Ali from Corvo

In the 15th century, an unmarried woman lived on the Azorean island of Corvo. She had a son called Alípio, whose darker skin color made him stand out among the rest of the population. Normally, unmarried women who happened to become pregnant were instantly expelled from the island, but this woman stayed and was consequently seen as a witch who was said to possess magical powers.

One can easily imagine how miserable her son's childhood must have been, given the social prejudices and general animosity mother and son had to face on a daily basis. Not even the children gave young Alípio any reprieve, and on one occasion, a stone thrown in a bitter dispute hit his right cheekbone so hard that a star-like scar tarnished his face for the rest of his life.

When one day pirates attacked the island, as they had done so many times before, young Alípio did not run away and hide with the other inhabitants of Corvo. He had made up his mind to join their gang instead. Happily he sailed away with them, and when after a rough journey, they landed in Tunis, Alípio was handed over to a fakir, who renamed him Ali.

Diligently, the young apprentice submitted himself to the strenuous and ascetic discipline of his demanding master. Through obedience and discipline and the acquisition of perfected intellectual skills, he aimed to achieve indestructible powers. As a sign of accomplishment, a chain with a pentagram pendent finally adorned his chest. Yet, the aspiring young magician yearned for infinite glory and riches. Clearly he remembered his mother's words: "Poverty is not a sign of disgrace, but rather an act of willful mischief."

Yearning for daring action, the ambitious Ali once again joined a gang of pirates and guided by a Muslim fatalistic spirit, submitted his fate to God/Allah. Soon after, the pirates set sail in two ships. They chose Ali as their captain, and he chose the distant Azorean island of Corvo as their first destination.

Yet, when they finally caught sight of the little island, the aspiring young pirate found himself caught in an emotional turmoil. Initially, Ali had set off to avenge his long-suffering mother. Now the grown Alípio remembered with fondness that Corvo had also once been home in his childhood.

Since he knew the island like the back of his hand, the pirate captain from Corvo had the two ships anchor in a lonely bay, where he had often used to go fishing and swimming without being pestered by the other children. Lost in his thoughts, the reminiscing Alípio did not notice a woman hiding behind a boulder. She had been collecting limpets and had spotted the two ships, immediately assuming that they must be pirate ships. Quietly, she slunk back to the village and raised the alarm, warning everyone of the pirate invasion.

The islanders did not waste any time, and since they could anticipate which way the pirates would use to raid the island, they rushed to the top of the surrounding hills and hid up there. They did not have to wait long for the pirates to come, and they certainly caught them by surprise, flinging stones and hurling rocks down at them, until the invaders decided that retreating was the only possible option to avoid being bludgeoned to death.

Out of breath, the pirates hastened back to where they had left their ships. However, the wind had picked up in the meantime, and both ships had slipped out of their mooring. One had been smashed against the reef, while the other one was drifting far out at sea. Menacingly, the pirates turned to face their captain. Had he led them to this island of his birthplace to deliberately betray them?

The angry shouts of the islanders pursuing the pirates grew louder. The wild sailors did not wait to clarify their doubts. A dagger glinted in the sunshine, and Ali's severed head fell onto the beach.

Hastily, the pirates swam to their remaining ship and miraculously escaped unharmed. The body of their former captain was seen to be drifting in the ship's wake as it set sail and left. His head, with eyes wide open, was staring up at the inhabitants of Corvo, when they came rushing to the beach. They thought his face looked familiar. But when they spotted the star-like scar on the right cheekbone, they knew that this fierce-looking pirate had once been unfortunate Alípio.

His head was buried on the beach, but the next morning they found it had once again been washed up by the tide and was rolling among the pebbles. Two more times did they try to put Alípio's head to rest, but each time the ocean washed it ashore again. People say that for years it rolled among the pebbles and boulders. And, thus, the sad fate of this unhappy pirate from the island of Corvo turned into a manifold warning.

Our Lady of the Rosary and the pirates

In the 16th century, the smallest Azorean island, Corvo, looked like a natural fortress with its steep cliffs and rugged coastline. Unfortunately, its natural harbor was conveniently accessible to traders and pirates alike. As the pirates did not shy away from taking advantage of this natural invitation, the inhabitants of Corvo finally resorted to moving their houses onto the cliff top, where they huddled around the little chapel.

One beautiful day, the inhabitants of Corvo were busy with their daily shores, the men working in the fields or tending their sheep, the women treating the wool or weaving at home, when, all of a sudden, a large group of pirates entered the harbor and started ransacking whatever they could find.

Hastily, the inhabitants retreated to the cliff top and resorted to hauling stones and dropping them onto the attackers. The corsairs wasted no time, and aimed their ammunition straight up in the direction of the frightened islanders. In utter despair, the assaulted inhabitants sought reassurance and help from the statue of Mary in the chapel behind them. They carried the statue of Our Lady of the Rosary right to the edge of the cliff. There she swayed slightly, mildly smiling down on the fiercely fighting pirates. Undoubtedly, the attackers were becoming increasingly desperate, as most of their ammunition aimed upwards inadvertently fell back down, causing serious injuries among the marauders. The emboldened islanders hurled down everything they could lay their hands on, thus not giving the pirates any reprieve. Finally, the wild corsairs had enough and clambered back into their boats. For some time, they did not dare to return to this island, where the smiling statue of Mary possessed the magical powers to ward off their ammunition.

Meanwhile, the inhabitants of Corvo renamed their statue of the benevolently smiling Mary, calling her Nossa Senhora dos Milagres, as she had indeed worked wonders to defend them from the fierce pirates. Today, you can still find the statue at its place of honor in the main church of Corvo.

The Holy Spirit appeases the ocean

The harbor of the smallest Azorean island, Corvo, was a natural harbor close to the mills. As commerce grew, the islanders needed more space for ships and boats and created a new harbor, Porto Novo. The harbor was used to import and export the island's produce, mainly cattle and wheat.

However, when the weather turned bad, nature wasted no time in reminding the inhabitants of Corvo and the nearby island of Flores that, in spite of all of their ingenuity, they remained humble souls tossed around in the middle of an unpredictable Atlantic Ocean. Not long after the first settlers had established human ties between the two communities on the islands, a fierce winter storm made a late appearance just when May was about to give way to June; the Holy-Spirit-festivities had already started and everybody was already expectantly waiting for the mild breezes of summer.

The traffic in Corvo came to a complete standstill, and the people of Flores were left waiting for the oxen, which they needed for the Holy-Spirit-festivities. Even the *mordomo*, the responsible steward of the Holy-Spirit-festivities from Flores, found himself unexpectedly marooned in Corvo. He had intended to oversee the shipping of the cattle for the Holy-Spirit-dinner from one island to the other, but now there was no way one could even get close to the water. The gray sky was turning a darker hue as the day was threatening to come to a close. On both islands, the men approached the quays and stared across the general upheaval of waves and clouds, but not a glimpse of hope seemed to be in sight.

Desperation was about to set in, when all of a sudden, the *mordomo* of the Holy-Spirit-festivity resolutely stepped close to the waterfront. He calmly surveyed the rolling waves crashing against the coastline, and looked into the darkening sky, where the billowing clouds were chasing one another. When he spoke, his voice could clearly be understood above the din of the ravaging storm: "Load the cattle into the boat!" At first, the men around him thought they had not heard right. Then they protested and pointed out that in this kind of weather, cattle and men were doomed to be swept overboard and perish.

The steward turned to them and reasoned that, as the oxen were needed for the Holy-Spirit-festivity, the Holy Spirit would certainly look after them. The other men still thought this to be a crazy venture, but they obeyed and lowered the cattle into the boat. The women huddled together, wailing and moaning.

No sooner had the boat left the harbor, than the waves calmed down and the wind lost its force. The spectators on both islands held their breath, totally perplexed. Some crossed themselves, some whispered: "Praise to the Holy Spirit!"

The oxen reached their port of destination unharmed. The inhabitants of Ponta Delgada on Flores were delighted. Without these cattle, there would not have been the traditional meat dishes served to feed everyone at the Holy-Spirit-dinner. During the celebrations, the faithful thanked the Holy Spirit until the last morsel was eaten.

The Holy-Spirit-Crown

Right from the beginning of the first settlements, the boats between the neighboring islands of Flores and Corvo in the northwest of the Azorean archipelago helped transport goods and allowed relatives and friends to visit each other. As short as the distance between the two islands seems to be, just as unpredictable does the ocean prove to be at any given day of the year.

One sunny morning, a boat full of excited passengers looking forward to taking care of whatever they were planning to do on the little island of Corvo set off from the harbor of Santa Cruz in Flores. By the time their boat had covered half the distance between the islands, billowing clouds were chasing each other across the menacing sky. Angry waves were tossing the boat up and down so much that its passengers were losing every desire to cross over to Corvo. The ship's master realised how difficult it would be to anchor safely in the harbor of Porto Novo and attempted to disembark on a little quay. He was hoping that, sheltered by the island, the boat could get closer to shore.

At this moment, the inhabitants of Corvo who were overlooking the boat's plight from the cliff top above the port, got an idea. If anybody possessed power over the unleashed elements of nature, it undoubtedly was the Holy Spirit. They rushed to fetch the silver crown used during festivities, and, daringly, stretched out their arms over the edge of the cliff, the howling wind tearing at their hands holding the crown.

The crown glistened in the drenching spray – and, suddenly, the clouds careened eastward. The waves calmed down, and the sun shone again in a sparkling blue sky. The unfortunate boat landed safely in Corvo, and its adventure is still being recounted centuries later. There is no doubt in anybody's mind that it is by the grace of the Holy Spirit that the Azoreans can survive in the midst of the wild Atlantic Ocean.

Bibliography:

Almanaque Popular dos Açores.

Ângela Furtado Brum, Açores, Lendas e outras histórias, Ribeiro & Caravana, Ponta Delgada, 1999.

António Cordeiro, História Insulana das Ilhas a Portugal Sujeitas, no Oceano Ocidental, Secretaria Regional de Educação e Cultura, Terceira, 1981.

António Lourenço da Silveira Macedo, História das Quatro Ilhas que Formam o Distrito da Horta, (Reimpressão fac-similada de edição de 1871), 1981.

Archivo dos Açores.

Boletim do Instituto Histórico da Ilha Terceira.

Carreiro da Costa, Etnologia dos Açores, Rui de Sousa Martins, Lagoa, 1985.

Dante Caytano, Archipélago dos Açores, Nova Dimensão, 1987.

David Cordingly, Piraten: Furcht und Schrecken auf den Weltmeeren, VGS, Köln, 1999.

David Cordingly, Unter schwarzer Flagge. Legende und Wirklichkeit des Piratenlebens, Deutscher Taschenbuch – Verlag, München, 2001.

Douglas Stewart, Piraten. Das organisierte Verbrechen auf See, Mare-Verlag, Hamburg, 2002.

Fr. Agostinho de Monte Alverne, Crónicas da Província de S. João Evangelista das Ilhas dos Açores, Instituto Cultural, Ponta Delgada, 1961.

Francisco A.N.T. Gomes, A Ilha das Flores: Da Redescoberta à actualidade, Câmara Municipal de Lajes das Flores, 1997.

Francisco de Athayde M de Faria e Maia, Capitães dos Donatários (1439-1766), Instituto Cultural, Ponta Delgada, 1988.

Francisco F. Drummond, Anais da Ilha Terceira (Reimpressão fac-similada da edição de 1864), Governo Autónomo dos Açores, 1981).

Gaspar Fructuoso, Saudades da Terra, Instituto Cultural, Ponta Delgada, 2005.

João Marinho dos Santos, Os Açores nos Secs. XV e XVI, Serafim Silva, Maia, 1989.

José de Torres, Archivo Pittoresco, I-III, 1854-1857, Ponta Delgada.

José Rodrigues Ribeiro, Dicionário toponímico, ecológico, religioso e social da Ilha Terceira, Direcção Regional dos Assuntos Culturais, Angra do Heroísmo, 1998.

José Viale Moutinho, Lendas dos Açores, Esferado Caos Editores, 2007.

Manuel Ferreira, Ponta Delgada, Nova Gráfica, 1992.

Manuel Greaves, Histórias que me contaram, Horta, 1948.

Marcelino Lima, Anais do Município da Horta, Famalicão, Horta, 1940.

Marcus Rediker, Villains of All Nations, Atlantic Pirates in the Golden Age, Beacon Press, Boston, 2004.

Maximiliano de Azevedo, Histórias das ilhas, A.M. Perreira, 1899.

Núcleo Cultural da Horta, O Faial e a Periferia Açoriana nos Sécs. XV a XIX, Horta, 1995.

Peter Linebaugh, Marcus Rediker, The Many Headed Hydras, Sailors, Slaves, Commanders and the Hidden History of the Revolutionary Atlantic, Beacon Press, Boston, 2005.

Robert C. Davis, Christian Slaves, Muslim Masters. White Slavery in the Mediterranean, the Barbary Coast, and Italy, 1500-1800, Palgrave MacMillan, New York, 2004.

Azorean Legends as Folklore

Contents:

Foreword:

The oven that was spared from the fire

The bean pudding of the monks in Horta

Which sacristy X?

Flores

Our Lady of the Pirates or Our Lady of Ships

How the village "Caveira", Skull, got its name

How the "Cana da India" found its way to Flores

The mermaid of Ponta Ruiva

The tragedy at the Abyss of the seven Marias, the Baixa das Sete Marias

The legend of the dry pond or "Caldeira Seca"

The seven ponds of Flores

Corvo

The pirate and fakir Ali from Corvo

Our Lady of the Rosary and the pirates

The Holy Spirit appeases the ocean

The Holy-Spirit-Crown

This book is dedicated to

José Homem de Meneses
-    who harbors the Azorean soul in his heart.

I would like to thank Kika Monjardino for providing valuable insights into the intricate Portuguese language, and I want to give special thanks to my long-time friend Carol DeVore for volunteering her professional help with the English translation.

Maria Ângela Azevedo Furtado-Brum lived on the island of Pico until age 14, and then moved to Faial to attend high school, after which she lived and studied in Canada. In 1979 she returned to the Azores to live and teach at schools and at the university in Ponta Delgada on São Miguel, while she co-authored various school books. In the late 1980s Maria Ângela Azevedo Furtado-Brum started collecting the traditional stories and legends of the nine Azorean islands, which were published as *Açores, lendas e outras Histórias* and *Contos Tradicionais Açorianos.*

Regina Oberschelp de Meneses was born in Germany, where she studied to be a teacher of German and English. She taught at Scottish schools and then American universities, where she earned her PhD. Regina Oberschelp de Meneses also taught at various public and private institutions in Germany and Portugal and, in 1991, moved to the island of Terceira in the Azores, where she has been teaching at the university and various schools. She initiated a student exchange with German choirs at the EBS Tomás de Borba and the publication of the Azorean calendars "Edelsteine des Atlantiks" with photos by Paulo Henrique Silva (Amazon, Thalia).

Zeitfracht Medien GmbH
Ferdinand-Jühlke-Straße 7
99095 Erfurt, Deutschland
produktsicherheit@kolibri360.de